G. Knowles

KT-220-315

Effective Provision for Able and Exceptionally Able Children

Practical help for schools

Valsa Koshy and Ron Casey

WITHDRAWN

WS 2245723 2

371.95 KOS

NIS

Hodder & Stoughton

A MEMBER OF THE HODDER HEADLINE GROUP

UNIVERSITY OF CHICHESTER

British Library Cataloguing in Publication Data

Koshy, Valsa
   Effective provision for able and exceptionally able children
   1. Gifted children – Education
   I. Title II. Casey, Ron
   371.9'5

   ISBN 0 340 67945 X

First published 1997
Impression number   10 9 8 7 6 5 4 3 2 1
Year   2000 1999 1998 1997

Copyright © 1997 Valsa Koshy and Ron Casey

All rights reserved. No part of this publication may be reproduced or
transmitted in any form or by any means, electronic or mechanical, including
photocopy, recording, or any information storage and retrieval system, without
permission in writing from the publisher or under licence from the Copyright
Licensing Agency Limited. Further details of such licences (for reprographic
reproduction) may be obtained from the Copyright Licensing Agency Limited,
of 90 Tottenham Court Road, London W1P 9HE.

Typeset by Wearset, Boldon, Tyne and Wear.
Printed in Great Britain for Hodder & Stoughton Educational, a division of
Hodder Headline Plc, 338 Euston Road, London NW1 3BH by Bath Press, Bath.

Contents

About the authors

Valsa Koshy and Ron Casey have extensive experience as teachers in both primary and secondary schools, where their work with higher ability pupils alerted them to the need for research into effective educational provision. They are the co-directors of the Brunel Able Children's Education Centre at Brunel University, the first centre of its kind within a university providing in-service training for teachers and conducting research into curriculum provision for the able. The authors' publications include *Bright Challenge* and *Making Information Technology Work for You* from Stanley Thornes, and *Effective Teacher Assessment* from Hodder & Stoughton.

Acknowledgements

We would like to thank all the teachers who have attended our in-service courses on educating higher ability pupils; in particular teachers from Cambridgeshire, Kensington and Chelsea, Lambeth, Richmond, Southwark, Surrey and Wandsworth who have helped us to develop our thinking.

We would also like to thank our colleagues at Brunel University for their support and appreciation of the complexity of the topic of this book, and for giving us constant encouragement.

We are very grateful to all the children who have worked with us, for the hours of pleasure they have given us and for the very special pieces of work they have allowed us to reproduce in this book.

We would like to thank OfSTED for allowing us to reproduce Figure 1.1 from their publication *Exceptionally Able Children* (1993), Stanley Thornes for giving permission to reproduce activity sheets from *Bright Challenge* and Richmond LEA for letting us use an example of scientific thinking in Figure 5.6, which is in its trialling stage at present.

Introduction

Throughout *Effective Provision for Able and Exceptionally Able Children: Practical help for schools* we offer the reader a framework to consider many of the aspects relating to the identification, nurture and fulfilment of special abilities and talents of the children in our care. The content of this book is based on our practical involvement with a large number of children and teachers over many years, and we hope it will be of interest and relevance to you. We invite you to join us on an interactive journey to explore the issues relating to educating higher ability pupils. During that journey, you should feel excited and sufficiently motivated to take on the challenge of finding out more about the education of our most able pupils, which we believe is one of the most complex aspects of education. We have campaigned passionately for a fair deal for our able pupils over a long time, and we hope our experience will make *you* feel more confident to offer guidance and leadership to your colleagues.

We begin the book by setting the context of the exploration, in Chapter 1, by providing a background to the identification and provision for the most able pupils in our schools. We argue that this area of education is very important and we believe it has been long neglected. We provide evidence that some of the brightest children in our schools are disadvantaged, from HMI reports and surveys, OfSTED reports and from our own research and experience. We present a list of what schools are 'expected' to provide and invite you to make reflective appraisal of the state of the art in yours as well as in your personal development. In preparation for your exploration, we will provide you with a list of objectives for your school or institution. In this chapter we also address issues relating to the different terminology used to describe high ability, and about labels and ways in which ability is often assessed and identified. These are explored with the help of case studies of children and adults we have either worked with or with whom we have had direct contact. These should help the reader to focus on the different issues which provide an appropriate background.

In Chapter 2 we invite you to reflect on your own perceptions of what constitutes 'higher ability' as well as provide you with an overview of the perceptions of others – researchers and educationists – on what constitutes higher ability. We present some theoretical models of higher ability to enable you to consider. The complex issue of identification of higher ability pupils is discussed and we propose many methods and record systems within the existing structures of a schools' organisation with which you can make valid and fair identification of ability. A checklist of characteristics which may be displayed by higher ability pupils, drawn on our experience, is provided as a guide to support you in the process of identification. With the help of classroom examples of children's responses to work and some tangible products we encourage and assure you that effective provision for higher ability pupils is within everyone's reach. Before concentrating on effective classroom provision for these pupils we take a close look in Chapter 3 at what we think their special needs are.

Through the use of examples, both the affective and cognitive needs of these pupils are discussed and the reader is invited to consider what action may be necessary to meet them. The social and emotional needs of higher ability pupils are also considered, along with a discussion of how teachers can provide a congenial environment for the fulfilment of their academic potential as well as encouraging these pupils to be well-rounded personalities. The characteristics of the 'best' teacher for higher ability pupils are also considered.

We believe that the most exciting and challenging aspect of educating the most able pupils is the aspect of curriculum provision, which is outlined in Chapter 4. Effective curriculum provision for these pupils does not happen by accident. We discuss aspects of provision using the CK model, which provides a model of considering provision in the classroom context. Terms such as 'differentiation', 'enrichment' and 'acceleration' are considered and examples are provided. Models of curriculum delivery are considered within the context of the National Curriculum. With the help of examples of teaching different age groups, we make some suggestions about how to make adjustments and modifications to the existing curriculum to make it more suitably stimulating for *all* pupils, including higher ability pupils. The incorporation of higher levels of thinking into the curriculum planning, and the role of challenging questions are discussed. We share some ideas on differentiating the curriculum based on a theoretical model, and invite you to implement the strategies in your everyday planning.

In Chapter 5 we ask the reader to share some experiences with us on how to design enriched curriculum materials for higher ability pupils. For the purpose of illustration we share our *Bright Challenge* (1995) experiences of designing extended projects and curriculum materials for children within the context of the National Curriculum. A set of principles are introduced and examples of how these have been put into practice are provided.

In Chapter 6, the final chapter of the book, we try to highlight aspects which make a difference to effective provision for the most able pupils. The design of a school policy for meeting the needs of the most able pupils, we believe, can make a difference to the effectiveness of the provision. Guidance on what to include in a school policy, as well as examples of two policies from two different phases of schooling, are provided, along with suggestions for a series of in-service sessions in order to prepare the teachers to design their policy with a greater understanding of the issues. A list of useful contacts and support organisations is provided at the end of the book, followed by a Bibliography of what we consider would make useful reading.

We have written this book in an interactive style in order to facilitate reflection on issues. At different points we ask you to be engaged in some discussion with colleagues or in deliberations within yourself. Although these 'engagements' are optional, we believe that the topic of this book – how to identify and provide effectively for the most able pupils in our schools – is one of the most complex issues and time spent in rationalising all aspects of the topic should enrich both your pupils and yourself.

CHAPTER *1*

Able and Exceptionally Able Children

Background

The recognition that pupils of higher ability exist in all schools, and that the needs of these pupils should be met, are not new concepts. Educationists and researchers, both in Britain and abroad, have long been engaged in studying aspects of high ability. Their studies have provided us with much guidance on how to begin considering issues relating to effective provision for higher ability pupils. However, it is worth mentioning that there has been less research carried out in Britain than in many other countries. Much useful literature has been available from the USA, where several million dollars are spent on 'gifted' education every year and much of this funding is provided from government sources. This literature has provided us with useful starting points and some of these will be referred to in this book.

In Britain over the last fifty years, many perspectives with regard to aspects of higher ability education have enriched our knowledge of this area of education as well as provide us with a forum for debate and reflection. However, in the last five years there has been an increased awareness of the need to address the education of our more able students. This awareness has been manifested through the increased number of new publications and of one-day conferences, and many local education authorities are now in the process of producing policies to address issues relating to the education of very able pupils. Many schools are seeking help to design school policies, and often this is in response to a substantial number of OfSTED inspections pointing out the schools' inadequacy in providing a suitable education for their most able pupils.

What do we need to do?

So what are the schools expected to provide? Three clear messages were put forward in the 'Schools Update' (1994). They are summarised here:

- It is important that schools identify gifted children within their development plans and that clear objectives in this aspect of education are located within schools' broader policies.

- General and subject criteria developed by schools are crucial in helping teachers to identify high ability.

- Ensuring that one teacher in each school has responsibility to co-ordinate for the most able is a critical factor in ensuring that good practice is disseminated and extended.

Perhaps this is a good place for you to start your journey. Think for a moment about the three criteria listed above – from the standpoint of the role you presently hold in your school (be it class teacher, subject co-ordinator or head of department, special needs co-ordinator or headteacher) – and make a judgement on where you are with regard to the three messages above. Does your school have a policy for 'able pupils'? Have you got a co-ordinator responsible for the education of high ability pupils? Does your subject teaching policy include a statement about the identification and provision for higher ability students in the respective subjects? It may be that your school has made quite a lot of progress in all the three areas, or it may be that 'higher ability children' is one of the priority areas in your school development plan. You may find Figure 1.1 opposite useful for reference as this is provided by OfSTED (1993, p. 11) as a useful framework. Whatever state your school is in at present, read on to develop your expertise.

Why should we care?

There are many reasons why we need to address the needs of the most able pupils in our schools. There can be no doubt that identifying the talents and strengths of the most able and nurturing these talents is of tremendous economic importance, as our children are the most precious resource we have for our future. In the technologically advanced and competitive world we live in, our survival and prosperity depend on having the alert and capable minds of our children involved in creative thinking and problem solving.

Next, there is the right of each individual child. All children are entitled to be recognised for their talents and special aptitudes; they are also entitled to the kind of

Inspection

The revised framework for the Inspection of Schools, under the heading of 'Equal Opportunities', defines the core task as assessing the influence of the school's practice and policies on pupil's access to the curriculum and their achievements. 'Giftedness' is included under this heading as are ethnicity, bilingualism, gender and social circumstances.

There are a number of basic questions which I would like to see the inspection teams address.

- Does the school have any policy or guidelines covering the needs of the most able children?

- What steps are taken to identify high ability or to diagnose underachievement (for example, use of standardised tests, checklists)?

- Is use made of regular assessment procedures to identify high ability or underachievement?

- Does the way in which teaching groups are organised facilitate differentiation of work according to ability?

- Is any special provision made for the very able either within normal classes or through withdrawal for enrichment activities?

- Are there any pupils in the school who have been promoted ahead of their chronological year or who have been accelerated in individual subjects?

- Are there references to the needs of very able children in the subject schemes of work?

- Are any pupils engaged in enrichment schemes which are provided for very able pupils by the LEA or by outside organisations? Is there any feedback and/or follow-up to these schemes?

- Have any links been established with other schools, further education institutions, universities, colleges of higher education, local businesses and industry or with members of the community in order to provide enrichment or extension for very able pupils?

- Is there a named co-ordinator for able pupils?

- Is any staffing time targeted specifically on the needs of very able pupils?

- Has any relevant in-service training taken place in recent years?

Figure 1.1 An extract from HMI McIntosh's speech (OfSTED, 1993)

education which supports the development of their full potential. Having the necessary structures for the development of potential in place in every school is really all about fairness and equity, because it makes it possible for *all* children to have the opportunities to make use of their talents, not just the few who may be privileged to have adults at home who have the time, knowledge, interest and resources to support their development.

From an educational point of view, many teachers have consistently pointed out to us that by focusing on higher ability pupils they have found a general improvement in the standards of all pupils. Barbara, a class teacher, explained this clearly:

It was not until I started to focus on planning what was appropriate for the most able pupils in my class that I realised that almost everything I used to plan was targeted at the average pupil. When pupils completed their work, I moved them on to more 'similar' work where the emphasis was not always on quality, but on quantity. I made sure that the most able pupils always had work to do to keep them busy ...

HMI (1992) expressed a similar view, based on their survey of provision for very able pupils in primary and secondary schools. They maintained that where specific attention is given to able children there is often a general increase in the level of expectation for all pupils and this is sometimes reflected in improved public examination results.

Making sense of terminology

Whenever the issue of adequate provision for able children is being considered, one question often asked is about the 'type' of pupils being referred to. Who are we talking about? People often refer to able children using a number of diverse terms – *able*, *very able*, *gifted*, *bright*, *exceptionally able*, *talented* and *intelligent* are just a few of them. Parents, teachers and others also seem to possess their own images attached to these terms. While we believe there are more able pupils than suspected in every classroom and some of them may possess exceptional capabilities, using pre-set definitions and images are unlikely to provide effective strategies for dealing with real issues. In this book we ourselves refer to 'higher ability' pupils, 'exceptionally able' pupils, 'most able pupils' and so on, which prompts us to deal with the issue of labelling and use of terminology early on.

You may have heard of the suggestion that only a very 'small percentage' of pupils are 'gifted' and that the needs of these pupils can only be met if they are educated separately. Quite often reference is made to IQ (Intelligence Quotients) scores to describe how 'intelligent' a person is and how that person may be among the top

0.5 or 1% of the population. Percentage scores are sometimes used to create cut-off points, at 25% of the children being 'able', the top 5% being 'exceptionally able'. It is also quite common to use the term 'talented' to refer to children who possess special aptitudes in non-academic subjects. Along with many teachers in both secondary and primary schools, we do not believe that specific labelling or the use of percentages to describe groups of pupils in any way offers helpful strategies, either in the identification or provision for able children.

We think a more useful strategy is to view ability as a continuum, as is illustrated in Figure 1.2 (below). Instead of having an able and non-able group, it is better to think of the need to provide for the more able pupils as and when you recognise the need for a differentiated provision. This ability continuum consists of a straight line with a noteworthy feature: no points are indicated on it to show clear points of demarcation between the categories represented by the line.

Able   more able   exceptionally able

Figure 1.2   The ability continuum

Flexibility

Allowing for flexibility in assessing higher ability is important for many reasons. First, it encourages us to have enough humility to be aware of our own limitations in our identification strategies. Second, identification of abilities takes time; it is more effective under the right conditions. For example, it is important to provide an enriched curriculum which offers opportunities for children to show their talents. Without this it is likely that some of the most able pupils may not be identified at all. We were given the example of Daniel, aged 6, whose teacher was surprised to find out how exceptional his ability was with language when one day she asked her class to create a radio play. When she saw how outstanding his talent was, she told Daniel that she did not know he was 'so brilliant at making up plays'. He then admitted to not always 'finishing his work' on time because he did not find the work 'interesting'! If we were to offer a curriculum which is stimulating, with a balanced diet of activities which offer potential for pupils to be engaged in higher levels of thinking, it is likely that the labels we use won't matter. This does not, however, prevent a teacher seeking extra provision for those children who may exhibit exceptional talent. In many cases we find that with a flexible identification process and careful planning of the curriculum the needs of most of our higher ability pupils can be met within the classroom. In the following sections of the book we will share some of our experiences to illustrate our point.

The higher ability child

Think of the most able child in your class and write down a few phrases or words which describes to someone else the reasons why you have chosen that particular child. List some of the characteristics which led to you making this choice. A spider diagram like the empty one below may be useful to do this.

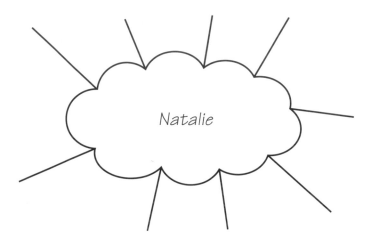

Natalie

If you have an opportunity to do this in a group, it is better still as it makes an interesting exercise for you to compare your list of characteristics with those of others afterwards. Are there similarities? On our in-service courses, we found some similarities in teachers' lists but not enough to generalise. Assessing higher ability is a complex process. The different interpretations given of what is meant by higher ability explains the difficulty in coming up with general rules. One aspect we regularly find is that the children chosen by teachers showed a substantial bias towards boys, and this is significant. What do you think the reasons are?

Figure 1.3 shows a spider representation provided by the teacher of a very able pupil we have come across. Does it have similarities with your list? It is possible that the characteristics listed here for Samantha are not what most people would often associate with an exceptionally able child. In the following sections we have included case studies of 6 people: 4 pupils from the primary age group, one adult and one secondary school pupil.

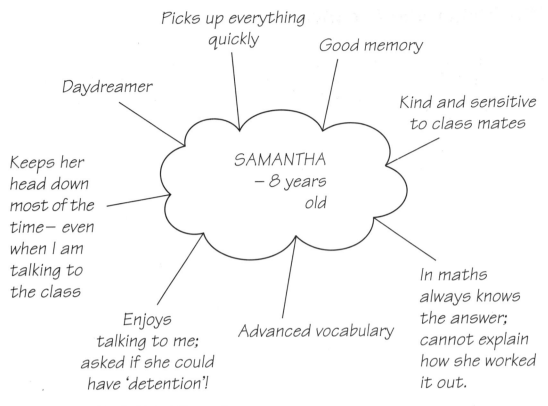

Figure 1.3   Profile of a high ability pupil

Case studies of six children

Although there are as many differences as similarities between the different cases of able and exceptionally able children we have come across, we have often found that teachers welcome the opportunity to consider the cases of different types of children in order to best understand ways of recognising them through the diversity of their behaviours and backgrounds, and in order to reflect on how best to provide for them. The following case studies were compiled with the help of class teachers who claimed that each of the people presented here posed real challenges. It is very likely that you will be able to relate types of children you have come across, in your school or classroom, to these case studies. After each of the cases we have raised some questions for you to consider, whether individually, in pairs or in a staff meeting.

The case studies that follow also serve another purpose. They may help you to understand issues discussed in later chapters, with real examples to assist you.

CASE STUDY 1 – Peter

Peter is ten years old. His parents had noticed his exceptional ability from a very young age. Among the early indicators of his ability was the way he learnt things very quickly, his use of sophisticated vocabulary and an unusual interest in Open University programmes (noticeable from the age of five). Both his parents were Oxford graduates. Peter's teachers also identified his high ability from the start. The school felt quite confident that they could keep Peter stimulated in the classroom. This changed when Peter was eight years old when, according to his teachers, it was clear that he was years ahead of the other children in his cognitive development. They then had to consider other strategies to teach him appropriate to his potential. The first solution offered by the school was to move him up three years to a Year 6 class where he would have no difficulty in coping with the academic work. His parents agreed. This was tried for a few weeks until one day Peter came home crying because he was not 'chosen' to be in the class football team because he was considerably 'shorter' than the rest of the class. He found no difficulty in doing the 'work' set for Year 6 children, but felt isolated due to being physically smaller. Peter was then moved to a Year 4 class where his difference in size was not so obvious and where he felt much happier.

Moving Peter to a class where he could work and socialise with children a year older did help, but meeting all his academic needs remained a challenge for Peter's new class teacher. She felt her own knowledge of all subjects – especially mathematics and physics – was not adequate to offer him the stimulation he needed.

Here we have an 'exceptionally' able pupil in most subjects, whose ability was easily spotted by both his parents and school. Both made conscious efforts to nurture his ability, although educating him posed a constant challenge.

Questions

- If Peter was in your school what indicators would you have spotted to identify his ability?

- What feelings would Peter arouse in you as his teacher?

- What strategies would you adopt in providing for him in your class? Think about both social and educational provision

- What do you think Peter's special needs are?

- How would you offer him a challenging curriculum and keep him happy and settled?

- Do you have a school policy for catering for pupils like Peter?

CASE STUDY 2 – Collette

Collette is six years old. During her early years she was a dreamer, both at home and at the playgroup. She was slow to walk and talk. Her parents, both professional people, watched with dismay as Collette would sit and watch television for hours and look at books for long periods of time. When she eventually started to talk, she tended to ask questions all day. But once she started school, the problem of Collette's day-dreaming escalated. She never completed any written work and sucked her thumb constantly. Other children laughed at her 'excessive' interest in the books on the teacher's desk. Her parents were told about the 'day-dreaming' and 'laziness' problem and the school suggested that Collette be referred to the school psychologist. As the waiting time to be assessed could be over a year, Collette's anxious mother decided to have her daughter assessed by a psychologist in the private sector. The psychologist's report contained the following comments:

Collette concentrated for the whole two hours while she was being assessed, taking just a short break to have a drink and biscuits. She talked with excitement and seemed to enjoy all the tasks given to her. Her reading age is at least four years ahead of her chronological age. Her problem solving ability is superior and her mathematics knowledge is advanced too. Her general IQ is 150 which puts her in the top 1% of the ability range.

Collette's mother took the psychologist's report to the school. The following day the headteacher took Collette into her room and did 'an hour's work' with her on how to make up word puzzles. Collette's enthusiasm and her capability to decode word puzzles and find alternate meanings was astonishing. This practice continued for a few months. Every day Collette went to the headteacher's room for an hour and worked on a range of topics. Her writing was very imaginative. The headteacher maintained that she could easily obtain a Level Four in the National Curriculum test, if her spellings did not let her down. Sometimes during the sessions, Collette sucked her thumb and stood on her head and fidgeted all the way. At the same time, the quality of her questions and work were outstanding.

Here is a case of a pupil who was not identified as an 'able' child by either her parents or teachers. Here we can see that an IQ test helped to identify the exceptional ability of a child possibly dismissed as being 'slow', 'dreamy' and underachieving.

Questions

- Which factors may interfere with the identification process?
- Do you consider high ability to be dependent on the child being articulate and conforming to the rules and routines of the class?

- Are there circumstances when an IQ test may be very useful?

- If you were Collette's class teacher, which strategies would you use to help her to reach her full potential?

- Is an hour a day with the headteacher a good solution?

- Which factors do you think may have contributed to Collette's new-found enthusiasm?

CASE STUDY 3 – Mick

Mick is in Year 5 in a suburban school. He works hard and produces work of a good standard. His mother recently visited his teacher and demanded to know what the school was offering Mick, her 'very able' son, as special provision 'like the school down the road' does. That school, she claimed, had special projects for 'gifted' children. Mick's teacher told his mother that he was one of the able children in her class and that he was performing at the right 'level' for his age in the National Curriculum. She did not consider that Mick needed any 'special' work, as she tries to give all the children in her class work appropriate to their abilities. Mick's mother then wanted to know how 'able' he was compared to the other able children in the class. She continued to visit the school, threatening to take him to another school, as well as complain to the LEA that her son's needs were not being met.

Here is a case of a mother wanting to measure 'how' able her son is in spite of being assured by the class teacher that 'how able' Mick is was not important to her. What was relevant was that he was working well and achieving. According to her, Mick was a happy child until his mother started to come to school wanting to know the extent of Mick's ability. He began to show nervousness and anxiety as a result.

It appears that Mick is an able child. The class teacher had recognised his higher ability and tried to reassure Mick's mother that knowing 'how able' Mick is didn't make any difference to the way she treated him or provided for him.

Questions

- Do you have parents in your school who insist on wanting to know 'how able' a pupil is?

- Does it help you as a teacher to know 'how able' a pupil is? Are there ways in which we could tell 'how able' a child is?

- Do you have structures in place to show that the curriculum you offer is suitable for the most able in your class and that every child is encouraged to achieve the best possible results without being labelled as 'able', 'very able', 'gifted' and so on?

CASE STUDY 4 – Jason

Jason is 19 years old and is currently working in a betting shop. He believes his secondary school failed him because 'they' never really realised that he had high ability. According to his parents, the school was situated in an urban, disadvantaged area where there were no high expectations. There were no efforts made by the school to identify the most able pupils and target them with help and encouragement. Jason believes he was a very capable mathematician who never 'had a chance to show his ability' because all the lessons were targeted at the average or below average pupils. The aspirations of most of the pupils were low and no one 'really cared'.

Now Jason feels that he was treated unfairly by a system which failed to recognise high ability independent of social status.

Questions

- Do you have a school policy which sets out procedures for the identification of very able pupils, regardless of background?

- Are you aware of the special difficulties associated with the identification of higher ability pupils in deprived areas, where pupils may have low self-esteem and their parents low expectations of them?

- Do you have structures in place to encourage high ability children to set targets for themselves?

CASE STUDY 5 – Rebecca

Rebecca, at 13, was described by her teacher as one of the best mathematicians the school has ever had as her ability was exceptional. The way the school provided for her was by entering her for GCSE Mathematics in Year 8. She obtained an 'A' grade. This was felt to be a remarkable achievement by all concerned, but Rebecca started having problems after passing her GCSE. She was extremely upset that she was stopped from having any more mathematics lessons, depriving her of the most pleasurable experience in her school day. The 11–16 school did not have the facility to offer her A Level lessons. She had to deal with other teachers' expectations, which Rebecca's parents described as 'unrealistic', to perform at a very high level in all subjects. Rebecca also had to endure teasing from other pupils for being the 'boffin', and this made her school life unbearable. Rebecca's parents took her out of school and educated her at home. A very bouncy, alert Rebecca became moody and unhappy. Her results at 16 were 3 GCSE passes. She felt if she had attended school she would have done better.

The strategy offered by Rebecca's school may have created more problems than it helped to solve, although it seemed that the school was trying to do the best for her.

Questions

- Do you expect your pupils to be 'very able' in all areas?

- What is your view of Rebecca's reward for being exceptional in mathematics (being deprived of studying mathematics earlier than everyone else)?

- What benefit did Rebecca gain from taking the mathematics GCSE early?

CASE STUDY 6 – Anna

Anna is nine years old and is 'very bright' according to her Dad, who approached us for advice on how to help her at home as well as giving her teacher some ideas on how to best provide for bright children. Anna's parents also wanted to find out 'how' bright she was and for this they enlisted the help of a psychologist to test her IQ. One morning came a telephone call from Anna's mother. The conversation was as follows:

Mother   I need advice, I am devastated about what happened to Anna.
Author   Please explain what happened. We will do our best.
Mother   I had Anna tested.
Author   Tested, and . . .
Mother   Yes, tested. You see, her IQ was recorded at 136. The man who tested her said that if her score was 140 or more, she would have been classified 'gifted'. Now I cannot go to her school and ask for special provision.
Author   I see, how is Anna different to you today, after finding out what her score is, to what she was yesterday? Is she less bright? Is she not capable of doing what she could do before? What purpose has the test served?
Mother   Can't you see she has just missed being 'gifted'. What are we going to do?

Anna's mother was not particularly pleased with our questions. But this case study highlights the dangers of relying on tests to classify children as 'gifted' or 'non-gifted'. What do a few marks or scores matter anyway? The difference in score – in Anna's case if she had obtained four more points – could not in any way help her teachers to provide for her differently.

- Does labelling children as gifted help the teacher or the child?

- If and when Anna finds out that she had 'just missed' being 'gifted', what effect could this have on her confidence and expectations? Might she feel she had let her parents down?

- If Anna's score was 142 instead of 136, what difference would it make?

- Do we ever describe someone as 'almost rich' because they do not have sufficient amount of money to be classified as rich?

Summary

What we have attempted to do through these case studies is to raise some issues about labelling children. We believe that for the practical purpose of educating children labelling and classifying children as 'able' or 'not able', 'very able' or 'not very able', 'talented' or 'not talented', 'gifted' or 'not gifted', serves no useful purpose. It is better to consider ability as a continuum and accept that higher ability exists in most classrooms. Being flexible and open-minded about our assessment is far more valuable than any predetermined labelling.

The six case studies in this chapter also show that children possess varying degrees of ability and in some cases their abilities may be displayed in specific areas.

CHAPTER 2

Identifying Children's Abilities

In the previous chapter we introduced some of our thoughts concerning the importance of being aware of children of higher ability in our schools, as well as the need to make adequate educational provision. With the help of case studies we tried to highlight some of the complexities involved in understanding the various items of terminology used and the obsession of many people with labelling children as 'very able' and 'not very able' as well as with determining 'how able' a child is. We suggested what we feel to be a sensible strategy – to view ability as a continuum and be flexible in your judgement of children.

One of the recommendations in the OfSTED documentation referred to in Chapter 1 is the need to identify higher ability children. For this to happen your school needs to have structures in place. Before suggesting ways of identifying higher ability we need to consider what we actually mean by higher ability.

Making a start

Ask yourself what you understand by 'higher ability'. You could canvass your colleagues too, collect all the definitions and compare them with the following, offered by other teachers:

- children who are performing at higher levels in the National Curriculum than is considered average for their age

- children with very high IQs

- children who are faster learners

- those who don't need their teachers to teach them

- children who know more than the teacher does

- children who are creative

- children who are very articulate and confident

- those who have outstanding talent in a specific area

- children who are on the teachers' conscience for not being given much teacher time

Each of the descriptions above tells part of the story from which you will be able to construct your own. This book should help you to do that by providing you with an overview of some of the existing practices and beliefs about the nature of ability. We will also draw on some theoretical models which try to explain 'higher ability'. The theories referred to are included with the intention of familiarising you with current thinking. Although no single theory or practice is being exclusively recommended, teachers often point out to us that this knowledge assists them to consider and adopt the most suitable and relevant ideas. From this powerful position they can construct their own theory and philosophy and put it into practice.

Intelligence Quotient (IQ)

When people talk about higher ability in terms of pupils or adults having high IQ scores they are referring to results obtained by psychometric testing, which provides a single score as a measure of intelligence. IQ tests are usually carried out by psychologists to assess ability. Different tests are available and it is common to think of an IQ score of 140 as an indicator that someone is 'gifted' (if one is using a test such as the Weschler Intelligence Scales).

Closely associated with IQ testing is the belief that the population can be represented by a normal distribution curve which, in turn, can be approximated by a bar chart representation, as shown in Figure 2.1 on page 16, which is symmetrical and perhaps easier to accept as a model for providing guidance about intelligence. The administration of IQ tests is recommended by some groups as the most accurate predictor of the potential for doing well academically. There are others who challenge the usefulness of attaching a number to a child and dismiss it as a pointless exercise. The latter group maintains that a high IQ does not offer any practical basis for educational strategy; neither does it predict higher ability in a particular discipline. You may recall the case of Anna, in Chapter 1, in whose case awarding an IQ score is misused and could easily dent the child's development, confidence and progress. The reliability of IQ tests, which are mostly convergent and culturally based, is often called into question thus negating their usefulness as indicators of higher ability. The question often asked is: could a child who is a creative and a divergent thinker resent the multiple choice nature of these tests or do less well because of his or her ability to think of different solutions and combinations of solutions which do not fit the expected answer?

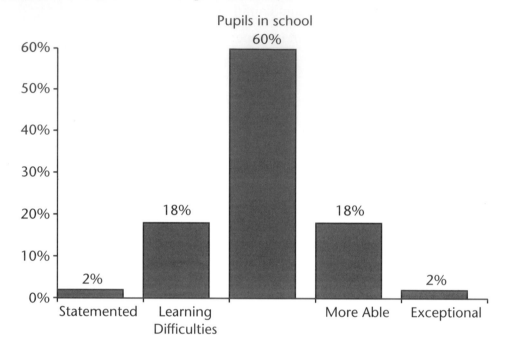

Figure 2.1 An approximation of an equal distribution curve

Areas of ability

During the past few years, both in the USA and Britain, there has been a move towards a more flexible view of the nature of higher ability and the way it is assessed. OfSTED (1993, p. 24) provides an example of how one local education authority uses special areas of abilities as guidance to assessing and registering abilities. They are:

- general intellectual ability
- specific academic aptitude
- creative or productive thinking
- leadership qualities/social skills
- artistic ability
- expressive arts
- physical ability

The above list is not unlike that put forward by Ogilvie (1973) after his search for a practical way of assessing higher ability in pupils. He offered a more flexible definition to include different areas of ability, rather than accept a narrower measure of a single dimension of potential.

The Renzulli Three Ring model

The definition of ability proposed by Renzulli (Renzulli and Reis, 1985), that higher ability pupils possess the capacity for or demonstrate high levels of performance in any potentially valuable area of 'human endeavour', is another move away from considering ability as a single dimension of potential. Renzulli proposes a useful model for practising teachers. He maintains that three factors – task commitment, above average ability and creativity – are essential for achieving higher levels of performance in a 'potentially valuable' area. His concept of the 'three ring model' of ability is presented in Figure 2.2 (below) and has much to offer in the ongoing debate on the nature of ability.

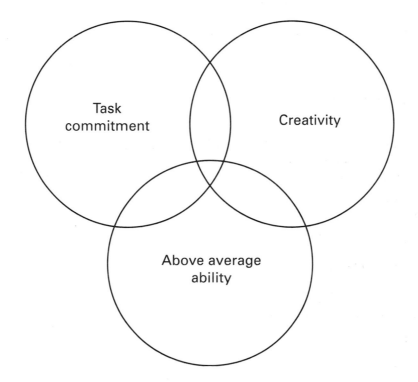

Figure 2.2 The Renzulli Three Ring model

Monks (1992) has added a social dimension to Renzulli's Three Ring model by proposing that the environment of the pupil – school, peers and family – influence the fulfilment of potential. This model is represented in Figure 2.3 (below).

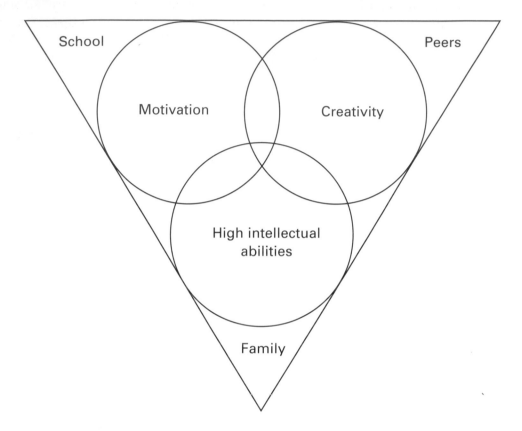

Figure 2.3   Possible influences on giftedness (Monks, 1992)

Within the framework of recent developments in the conceptualisation of higher ability, the importance of creativity has been stressed as an indicator. Like Renzulli, Sternberg and Davidson (1986) identified creativity as one of the three factors, along with commitment and intelligence, as important in any study of higher ability. Many recent studies have stressed considering creativity – the ability to think in a divergent way, being more flexible and possessing non-conformist ways of thinking – in terms of the nature of ability. This too has implications for us in the assessment of higher ability in our pupils.

Howard Gardner's Multiple Intelligences theory

The role of creativity is one of the aspects stressed as important by Howard Gardner, who has been involved in a number of educational projects in the USA. His theory of multiple intelligences has much to offer, which perhaps explains its world-wide acceptance. Many of the teachers we have worked with have been very enthusiastic about Gardner's theory of multiple intelligences, therefore we will devote some space to a discussion of it.

Gardner's theory (1983; 1993) rejects the notion of intelligence measured from the perspective of a single dimension, as it provides limited scope. He puts forward a list of seven intelligences which he believes offers a better framework to assess abilities. The seven intelligences are:

- linguistic intelligence
- spatial intelligence
- logico-mathematical intelligence
- bodily kinesthetic intelligence
- musical intelligence
- intrapersonal intelligence and
- interpersonal intelligence

Using examples of people who have made significant contributions in different fields, Gardner explains the seven types of intelligences. Our interpretations of these are given in the following section.

Linguistic intelligence

Those who possess this intelligence appreciate the order, meanings and rhythm of words. They are likely to enjoy the challenge of decoding the rules of grammar, inventing a new language, playing with words and enjoying communication. The life of T.S. Eliot (who created a magazine called 'Fireside' when he was ten years old, to which he was the sole contributor) is used by Gardner to illustrate linguistic intelligence. In a three-day period during his winter holiday the ten year-old Eliot created eight complete issues of the magazine.

Spatial intelligence

Gardner cites Pablo Picasso as an example of someone who possesses spatial intelligence. A person who is able to perceive the visual world and make representations of parts of it may possess this type of intelligence. The ability to create mental images and make use of them in unfamiliar circumstances is another feature of this intelligence. Art, design, architecture and navigation are likely to be the areas of excellence of such a person.

Logico-mathematical intelligence

Einstein is an example of someone possessing a high degree of logical-mathematical intelligence. Those who exhibit this type of intelligence are likely to be remarkable problem solvers; they may be experts at deduction and reasoning. They display powers of categorising, calculating, hypothesising, experimenting and developing logical arguments.

Bodily kinesthetic intelligence

Gardner explains this intelligence as the ability to use one's body to express an emotion (as in 'a dance'), to play a game (as in 'a sport') or to create a new product (as in 'inventing') – all evidence of cognitive features of body usage. Martha Graham, the dancer and choreographer, is used as an example of someone who possessed a high degree of bodily kinesthetic intelligence.

Musical intelligence

Those who possess this intelligence are sensitive to rhythm, pitch and timbre, and appreciate timing and tone. They enjoy creating and listening to music. Gardner provides the example of the internationally famous performer Yehudi Menuhin, whose remarkable gift for music manifested itself even before he touched a violin. His reaction to particular sounds and his rapid progress with the instrument as a child suggest that he was biologically prepared for this talent.

Intrapersonal intelligence

This intelligence is described as having access to one's emotions and the capacity to label and discriminate between them. Also to draw on them to guide one's own behaviour. These persons have a raised awareness of their strengths and weaknesses. Sigmund Freud is cited as representing this kind of intelligence. People with this kind of intelligence may be able to reflect more and be able to write more readily about their own feelings.

Interpersonal intelligence

Gardner describes this intelligence as the capacity to notice distinctions between people, such as contrasts in their moods, temperaments, motivations and intentions. This intelligence is likely to make one more empathetic and be a more effective leader and manager. These people are more likely to be good organisers and leaders of a community. The example of Mahatma Gandhi, who won the nation's love through non-violent protest, is provided as an example of someone with interpersonal intelligence.

You may agree with us that Gardner's Multiple Intelligences theory has strong implications for the assessment of abilities. He asserts (1993, p. 330) that understanding a profile of intelligences of a pupil is very useful in devising an educational programme:

Such a careful assessment procedure allows informed choices about careers and vocations. It also permits a more enlightened search for remedies for difficulties.

The implications of Gardner's multiple intelligences theory for the identification of higher ability children are discussed later in this chapter. For a teacher the significance of his theory for curriculum planning and organisation is certainly worthy of consideration.

Take a moment to remind yourself of the different viewpoints on both issues – the **nature** and **assessment** of ability. Make a list of key words to help you do that. Does your list include some of these?

single dimension tests   **creativity**

environmental influences   **task commitment**

IQ score   **Multiple Intelligences**

The diverse messages coming through the early sections of this chapter perhaps highlight the complexity of understanding the nature of ability. Identification of ability is not a simple process; nor is it clear cut. However, we hope we have provided you with some points for reflection on some of the issues.

If you remember the 'think of the most able pupil in your class' exercise in Chapter 1, we discussed the difficulty of establishing generalisable attributes to identify higher ability pupils. As teachers, you do need to know who the most able pupils in your class are, whether their talents are in a specific domain and what their needs are.

Whereas in the past there was much reliance on written and IQ tests to identify the 'able groups' of children, recent thinking and development in research about higher ability pupils, and how best to educate them, have encouraged us to employ a range of methods for identification. As this is a complex process, using as many ways as possible to make judgements about childrens' ability can only be a good thing. In the following sections we discuss the various options and opportunities available to us to achieve the most efficient method of identification. Gathering information from different sources can only strengthen the reliability of your judgements.

So what methods of identification are available to us?

1) The National Curriculum

Since the National Curriculum was introduced there has been more awareness among teachers of children's achievements in relation to their peer group. For example, a child who can deal with the content of the National Curriculum several levels ahead than considered average shows a capability to learn fast. Such learning and aptitude needs to be monitored and appropriate learning opportunities provided.

2) Teacher Assessment

Teacher assessment was introduced as a statutory requirement of the Education Reform Act of 1988. In consequence, more close observation procedures, continuous assessment and recording of children's learning have been introduced into schools. These procedures can lead to more effective identification of higher abilities. Teacher assessment is a much-favoured option for the identification of higher ability because teachers, along with parents, are in the best possible position to make judgements about children's ability and aptitudes. However, a word of caution needs to be added here. We cannot always assume that a teacher will be able to make a valid assessment of children's abilities, aptitudes or creativity if the opportunities are not provided for the children to manifest their abilities. For example, if a child's only mathematical work consists of doing pages of sums, it is not likely that the child will exhibit his or her powers of problem solving or logical reasoning. A linguistically talented child needs to be provided contexts in which his or her interest in vocabulary or grammar patterns may be explored for the teacher to be able to make valid assessment of ability.

So, when we say that teacher assessment is one of the most powerful ways of identification of ability, we make the assumption that enriched curriculum opportunities are provided for the pupils to show their ability.

3) SATs and other tests

As in the case of using teacher assessment to find out where a child is with regard to the National Curriculum content, results of Standard Assessment Tasks can often be indicators of higher ability. One teacher explained:

I will never forget the shock I had on the day seven year-old Matthew in my class did his SATS. In a quarter of the time everyone else took, he completed the test. A flabbergasted me gave him a test from a higher level; he did that too in twenty minutes. When I got over the shock, I told Matthew that I was very pleased with his work and asked why he did not do such good work every day to which he replied: 'Well, my mum told me we will be doing these tests this week, you see. I thought I better try hard.'

It seems that Matthew was a very capable child who chose not to show his ability at other times. The reasons for this can be speculated upon. We know of many cases where children do mask their abilities for fear of being asked to repeat the same type of exercises when they complete the assigned work. Tests published by NFER and other such organisations, which are standardised, are also used by some schools and authorities to identify higher ability pupils. Although these tests can be useful, in some cases the most able pupils are such divergent thinkers that their often 'creative' responses to questions may be 'wrong' according to answer sheets and can be considered 'weird' by their teachers. If a teacher is faced with this situation, a short diagnostic interview with the child may often produce surprises.

4) IQ tests

As mentioned previously, measuring intelligence using IQ tests has been used as a strategy for testing potential for a very long time. Through case studies we have shown that this kind of testing can be useful, as in the case of Collette who spent her time day-dreaming and apparently 'wasting' her time. We also know of other cases where pupils with apparent learning difficulties or disruptive behaviour have been tested and the potential predicted by the test score has been useful to the teachers and parents for identification purposes. Many of the tests used by independent schools to select pupils are similar to IQ tests. It is often considered that these tests can be good predictors of success in examinations.

5) Nominations

A strong partnership between parents and teachers has long been accepted as one of the factors influencing higher performance and the raising of achievements. It is only logical that schools should make an effort to communicate with the parents about the abilities and aptitudes of their pupils. An extremely valuable starting point for this would be to include some space, perhaps in application forms to the schools, to register these at the time of school admissions. Whilst one can often see a space for 'specific difficulties' on admission forms, only very rarely have we seen space allocated for pupils' strengths and special aptitudes. As self-assessment systems and Records of Achievement and portfolios are becoming more widely used, students' own nomination is also possible. Again, structures should be made available for pupils to record their strengths and special talents as part of the assessment system.

6) Using 'Identification' lists of characteristics

Although we are sure that you will agree with us that children who exhibit higher ability are diverse in their behaviour, so that generalising about their characteristics is an impossible task, many teachers have told us that they have found a list of pointers to identification a very useful starting point. Almost every conference you attend may provide you with a list of characteristics. The list in Table 2.1 opposite, which evolved from our experience of working with very able pupils who were nominated by teachers for participation in enrichment programmes, may be useful as a framework for observation of pupils in your class. As you read through each of them, take some time to reflect on the implications of each of these for the teacher and the school. We are often told, by teachers, that this is a worthwhile exercise. What does *your* list of implications look like so far?

The following example shows a teacher engaged in recording the implications for one of his pupils using this checklist. He reflected on one of his higher ability students, ten year-old Lisa, to help him focus on the ideas.

We feel this type of reflection is a good way of making use of identification lists. It may be that all your higher ability children will not show all the features listed, but they may show others. Only by making time and space available for this kind of thinking on how to identify and provide for the most able pupils, will we make any real impact on meeting the complex and important challenge of educating our higher ability children.

characteristic	implications
learns quickly	Lisa does not need to do 10 pages of multiplication sums. I know she can do them all in her head already.
is creative	I have several indicators of this, especially the book she made for me at home. I will give her the responsibility of displaying our topic work. She could do with learning to spell correctly and this will show her the 'real' need for correct spelling . . .

HIGHER ABILITY PUPILS

- often learn new ideas and concepts quickly or they may already know most of what they are being asked to learn
- may show dislike of repetition of concepts and of closed tasks
- are inclined to choose unusual methods of working
- are often reluctant to record things if they see no purpose in doing so
- may be creative in offering ideas and solving problems
- often show an unusual sense of humour
- may resent the imposed restrictions of the timetable if interested in a task
- display curiosity and ask more questions
- may be prone to being perfectionists
- are often capable of higher levels of thinking
- show more analytical thinking and reasoning
- may have a wider vocabulary
- may show interest in ideas and concepts which are often expected from an older group of pupils
- are often sensitive

Table 2.1 Some pointers to identifying higher ability pupils

7) Through observation of responses to questions and activities

Although the part played by teacher assessment has been discussed already, this section includes examples of some practical ways in which teachers have used good questioning skills and activities to assess their pupils through their responses. The examples of responses provided in Figures 2.4 and 2.5 on pages 26 and 27 show how they may help a teacher to make an assessment of her children's thinking styles and capacity to be engaged in higher levels of thinking. Let us look at the two examples.

Would you rather . . . ?

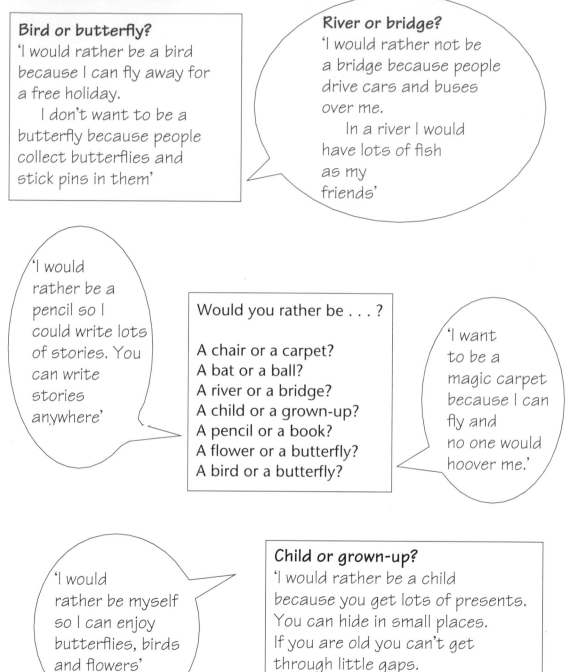

Bird or butterfly?
'I would rather be a bird because I can fly away for a free holiday.
   I don't want to be a butterfly because people collect butterflies and stick pins in them'

River or bridge?
'I would rather not be a bridge because people drive cars and buses over me.
   In a river I would have lots of fish as my friends'

'I would rather be a pencil so I could write lots of stories. You can write stories anywhere'

Would you rather be . . . ?

A chair or a carpet?
A bat or a ball?
A river or a bridge?
A child or a grown-up?
A pencil or a book?
A flower or a butterfly?
A bird or a butterfly?

'I want to be a magic carpet because I can fly and no one would hoover me.'

'I would rather be myself so I can enjoy butterflies, birds and flowers'

Child or grown-up?
'I would rather be a child because you get lots of presents. You can hide in small places. If you are old you can't get through little gaps. You live longer if you are younger'

Figure 2.4   Would you rather . . . ? Children's responses

Figure 2.4 contains five and six year-old's responses to questions based on the idea 'would you rather? . . .', collected by infant teachers as examples of children engaged in higher levels of thinking. In order to make responses to this kind of question, a child will need to be involved in a process of analysis and evaluation.

The second piece of work in Figure 2.5 was assessed by Zara's infant teacher to be of high quality and attributed to the production of this was the teacher's attempts to introduce higher order questioning skills.

Bird or Butterfly?   Zara 7 Yrs old

I want to be a butterfly.
I would like to be a Peacock butterfly.
I want to be a butterfly because I like their pretty colours and I can go on holiday without paying and you can fly very fast and butterflys can flit about. ButterFlys can sleep in flowers and sit on them. ButterFlys are symmetrical coloured. Butterflys can close their wings. ButterFlys can't be caught easily. ButterFlys are smaller than Birds.

Figure 2.5   Bird or Butterfly? by Zara, aged 7

8) Using a 'Multiple Intelligences' checklist

In many parts of the world checklists based on Howard Gardner's Multiple Intelligences theory are becoming increasingly popular to provide a framework for teachers' observations. The theory of Multiple Intelligences is a popular option because it focuses on and celebrates *all* talents and aptitudes, not just on the core curriculum subjects. If we believe that educating the whole child is important and encourages a multi-talented society which respects all abilities is a sensible way forward, then the basic framework for observation, as shown in Table 2.2 on page 28, is worthy of consideration. This observation schedule can be useful for identifying strengths in specific curriculum areas.

Name:

Linguistic intelligence
- Enjoys activities which involve working with words, spelling games
- Enjoys discussions, both factual and imaginative
- Enjoys reading and has an extensive vocabulary
- Shows competence as a creative writer in different types of writing: reports, stories, letters and poems
- Enjoys telling stories
- Shows interest in other languages and responds to the challenge of inventing languages

Spatial intelligence
- Shows aptitude for constructions, designs
- Awareness of space, pattern and layout
- Responds well generally to art and craft work
- Visualises details and perspectives

Logico-mathematical intelligence
- Shows enjoyment of mathematics
- Enjoys logic puzzles and capable of producing reasoned arguments
- Shows awareness of pattern and sequence
- Systematic problem solving abilities
- Good at hypothesising and generalising

Bodily kinesthetic intelligence
- Learns new sports with ease
- Uses body competently and with agility
- Well co-ordinated
- Very competent user of motor skills

Musical intelligence
- Enjoys musical activities
- Chooses to listen to music
- Strong awareness of rhythm, patterns and melodies
- Can reproduce new tunes and rhythms

Intrapersonal intelligence
- Shows initiative
- Knows own strengths and weaknesses
- Capable of having a laugh at oneself
- Empathises with other people's needs
- Reflective and can be easily engaged in self-evaluation
- Self-confidence

Interpersonal intelligence
- Shows management skills
- Shows sensitivity to others
- Co-operative in groups
- Shows leadership and organisational skills

Table 2.2 An observation schedule based on Howard Gardner's theory of Multiple Intelligences

Difficulties with identification

As we have reiterated many times already, the process of identification of higher ability is very complex. We have discussed the difficulties with the terminology used in relation to describing higher ability. 'What do you mean by a "higher ability" child?' and 'Do you mean a gifted child?' have been the most frequently asked questions. Statements such as 'I have never had a gifted child in my class in the last thirty years' are also common. Many people think of people like Gauss, the famous mathematician, or Mozart when they refer to giftedness. There is also the expectation that these gifted people had been outstanding pupils. This is not so. The most gifted pupils were not always identified as outstanding in their classrooms. There are many instances of very able adults either not being identified as capable when they were children or being misunderstood as disruptive pupils. Beethoven was apparently described as not having any musical gifts and Einstein as a 'dreamer' by their teachers!

Before concluding this section of identification of higher ability, we would like to share with you a list we put together for teachers on our in-service courses. Here it is.

Conditions which support effective identification of higher ability

- Provision of challenging classroom activities to enable the pupils to show aptitudes, quality of thinking and unusual conjectures
- Teachers' recognition of ability without being patronising
- Use of checklists which are carefully monitored and supplemented by other mechanisms
- Awareness of subject-based criteria of excellence
- A teaching style which fosters discussion and open-ended enquiry
- Careful recording of observed evidence of special abilities
- Opportunities for pupils to be engaged in self assessment, reflection and target-setting.

Summary

In this chapter we have looked at teachers' various definitions and interpretations of higher ability, urging you to construct your own story from a consideration of different concepts of what 'higher ability' entails. We have shared with you some well-known theoretical models, put forward by those who have studied the area of high ability. Ways of identifying high ability have been discussed. A list of structures which exists in the day-to-day life of your classroom, which can be used in the identification process, have also been provided.

As a result of reading this chapter it is possible you have already started looking at your pupils differently. You may have identified a 'lazy writer' as a talented playwright, a reluctant worker as a 'capable' mathematician. You may have forgiven a pupil who yawned out of boredom or decided that one of your pupils has so much interpersonal intelligence that he ought to be given the task of being the class 'arbitrator'! Our experience has shown us that teachers who make a conscious effort to look for special talents and aptitudes do find them – sometimes in the most unexpected cases. The next question to address is: 'what are these pupils' special needs?' Read on.

CHAPTER 3

Meeting the Needs of Higher Ability Children

Having considered the nature of ability and the different ways of assessing special abilities and aptitudes, we now focus on the special needs of higher ability children. We have no doubt that there is general agreement that the main purpose of education is to attend to the social, emotional and cognitive needs of all the children in our care. So, why is a chapter being devoted to the special needs of more able children?

Some of you may think that higher ability pupils are 'in any case, advantaged and privileged', so they should be able to look after themselves. This is not so. It may be true that to learn the basic curriculum these children may not need as much individual help from the teacher as other children do; but we believe that they too have their very 'special' needs. All higher ability pupils – whatever position they may occupy on the ability continuum – have needs which we must attend to. Again, trying to list those needs is not a simple task. For example, we think that 'exceptionally able' pupils have some special needs which are often difficult for most of us to appreciate. Some exceptionally able pupils may 'know' more than the teacher about a topic of special interest to them: teachers have often told us that it was beyond their conception how a five year-old can 'know' so much about planets or the names and characteristics of plants.

If you cast your mind back to Chapter 2 you may recall Lisa's teacher considering the criteria for identification of able children and reflecting on the specific needs of her own pupils based on that list. For example, a child who learns fast or who already knows most of what is being taught does not need to repeat several exercises from a textbook. That child may be frustrated by the lack of opportunities to become engaged in some kind of individual exploration at a deeper level. Similarly, the teaching style of the class – say mixed ability groups all the time – may be unsuitable for pupils who have special interests. These examples raise issues relating to teaching, but the needs of higher ability pupils in the context of other aspects of school life also need to be considered. We devote the following sections of the book to consider what we think are the most important special needs of these pupils.

Personal needs

Children spend a large part of their day in school and a great deal of their learning about the curriculum and life in general takes place there. In the school they find out what their capabilities and social responsibilities are. It is important the teacher recognises their special abilities and aptitudes so they can start building up their self-esteem and learn to give their best. Being accepted by their peer group in school is important in determining how they interact with others in their future lives. Case studies of adults and children, which have been the subject of substantial newspaper coverage, have reported that many higher ability pupils may be targets of teasing by peer groups. Our own experience of talking to parents suggests that there have been some tragic instances when the happiness and security of pupils was destroyed by teasing and bullying in the playground and classroom.

Sometimes teasing occurs when pupils show interest in unusual topics. We worked with four year-old Natasha who was obsessed with weather forecasts and the ozone layer. According to her parents, her peer group viewed her as 'weird' and it is not difficult to visualise their reaction when she expressed her legitimate concern for what may happen to us if we are not aware of the ozone layer and greenhouse effect. Natasha's teacher faced a real challenge – how to encourage Natasha to pursue her interests as well as get her classmates to accept she had an interest in something very worthwhile even if it was not something everyone else had to share and appreciate. What was remarkable was that as time went on, not only did the other pupils stop teasing and laughing at her, but some of her reception class started showing an interest in matters relating to atmospheric pollution and so on.

We know of very young pupils who, while playing with teddy bears and wanting constant hugs, show an interest in neural networks and nuclear physics at the age of six or seven. These are examples of children whose cognitive development was much more advanced in comparison with their physical development. These two examples are of exceptionally able pupils, but we have come across children who may be very able, though perhaps not exceptional, who have also been bullied by their classmates for 'getting everything right' and for working 'too fast'. In many cases the constant struggle to avoid teasing and bullying have turned some pupils off learning or stopped them wanting to go to school. Some parents have taken their children out of school and educated them at home. Although this is a course of action we do not recommend, when we have come across pupils whose parents have taken such action, we have felt saddened and frustrated by the desperate strategy being adopted.

This discussion does not overlook the fact that most very able pupils cope adequately in their class or school. We have enough evidence to show that where teachers recognise their pupils' higher abilities, and other pupils accept their often innovative and unusual thinking, this provides a very congenial environment for those pupils to be higher achievers as well as happier individuals. A good point to bear in mind is that we often see peer group adulation for children who exhibit aptitudes in music, drama and sport, but the same kind of admiration is not shown for academic aptitudes. Here is another challenge for the teacher!

'I don't want to be clever miss' behaviour

Among the many experiences shared with us by teachers, one that concerns us most is when pupils mask their abilities for either of two reasons. They may be afraid of peer group teasing, or they fear being given extra work which the other children may not have to do. Here 'being clever', they think, leads to being punished! A conversation which transpired between Janet, an infant teacher, and six year-old Matthew illustrates the point:

One morning at 9 o'clock Matthew greeted his class teacher:

Matthew   Miss, I am not going to do any more work for you, not ever again.
Teacher   Why is that Matthew?
Matthew   Because I have now worked out that I do more work than anyone else in this class and have less choosing time than everyone else. I love choosing time the best of all in school when I can build things and pretend to be a pilot and go on a space craft. I don't want to be clever miss.

Matthew was described as a very creative pupil by his teacher, who also felt 'terrible' that quite unintentionally she was loading 'too much' written work onto him when he completed his assignments. He always had to wait until others caught up. Such stories are common, although not many pupils would have expressed their resentment as Matthew did. The other point to consider is whether all teachers would listen to their pupils in the same 'patient' style as Janet did.

Another aspect is highlighted here. It is likely that Matthew, like many other infant pupils, articulated his feelings and frustrations more openly. Older pupils may not be so forthcoming with their views to enable teachers to take action. They may be afraid of displeasing their teacher.

In the light of what has been discussed, here are some questions for you to consider:

Questions

- Are the higher ability pupils in my care given a fair amount of my time to pursue their interests?

- How often have I considered whether some of my pupils may be targets of teasing at school?

- Do I make opportunities to discuss my most able pupils with their parents, or do I only speak to parents of pupils who have learning difficulties or are naughty?

- Do I praise my most able pupils or is praise 'reserved' for those who don't always produce excellent work?

- Is academic excellence always valued and celebrated in my class?

Learning needs

In this section we will focus on what we consider to be some specific learning needs of very able children. Closely related to learning needs are the implications for teaching styles.

Being independent learners

Many higher ability pupils enjoy pursuing their own interests. Within the framework of the National Curriculum this may seem to some as an impossibility. Yet in practice it *is* possible to find the time for these individual enquiries, by cutting out the time used for repetition of concepts and unnecessary revisions of the minimalist requirements of the prescribed curriculum. Quite often some higher ability pupils know much of it even before you start teaching them! While we believe it is right that a knowledge base offered through a statutory curriculum is a necessary prerequisite for higher ability pupils to be engaged in conducting enquiries, a curriculum based on accumulation of facts and skills only is likely to stifle curiosity and limit creative and innovative thinking – which our most able pupils are certainly capable of.

Being 'constructivist' learners

Over the last few years, we have had access to much literature focusing on learning styles, and there are two contrasting styles of learning which become targets of debate. The first is the 'transmission' model of learning, based on the belief that knowledge is passively received by the learner from what is 'told' by the teacher and others or found in books. The second is a 'constructivist' style of learning which is based on the belief that the learner constructs his or her own learning from a variety of sources.

A constructivist learning style is more reflective, includes much questioning from the self and from the teacher and may produce much conflict within oneself before new knowledge is accepted. Our contention is that while all pupils are constructors of their own learning, higher ability pupils are more likely to become engaged in questioning and modifying their structures of knowledge. Much of the teaching we have observed in schools consists of a passive style of learning. This is perhaps not surprising because a teacher has an obligation to teach her pupils basic facts and knowledge, and with large classes and other pressures she may feel finding time for reflection and evaluation is difficult. Or it may be that in the teachers' own training there was insufficient emphasis on how to encourage a reflective style of learning. The good news is that many teachers who have consciously tried to implement an active style of learning have commented on how much more powerful the learning and retention have been through this style of learning. The following comments from Laura, a Year 6 teacher, is representative of those comments:

Recently I have been trying to organise more time for my children to be engaged in an investigative learning style. I encourage them to ask more questions and spend time on thinking about what they are doing. I explain to them there is no need to have a tidy answer to every investigation. Most of the famous people we know about, I tell them, took several years to make their discoveries. After working on projects for several years, some scientists left only trails for others to follow and produce major inventions. The incomplete solutions are just as important in that they lead to significant contributions by themselves or for others to start from at a later date. It did sink in. I know because when I start telling them not to rush with their enquiries they quote back to me what I said to them – 'it doesn't matter if you don't finish it' and 'making mistakes is natural when you are thinking hard' and so on. When I reflect on my own secondary school days and the Masters' course I am presently doing, all the top grades are given to those who are reflective and analytical. Yet we don't encourage our young children enough to be engaged in these processes.

Whether investigative work is done in groups or individually, it is worth remembering that higher ability pupils are capable of much independent work and can be asked to complete a piece of work or project at home or in the library. It is useful to remember that many of the very able pupils may have a stronger knowledge base and many of them are more fluent and faster readers, thus capable of a great deal of research. They can be given special responsibilities for organising the research or for the final presentation of their work. This also serves the purpose of making them realise that their gifts and aptitudes can serve others, giving them the feeling of satisfaction of being appreciated by their classmates. This will provide training for them to reflect on their social responsibility of making use of their talents for the benefit of others too.

Being creative

A favourite quotation of ours about creativity is from Parnes (1963, p. 352):

Many people seem to possess seeds of creativeness but the environment fails to provide the proper nourishment for growth. Therefore, these people never fully live.

In the previous chapter we referred to aspects of creativity. We also believe that given the opportunities all children are capable of being creative to varying degrees, but, in our experience, some of our most able are capable of creating much of value if we provide them with opportunities to be creative.

The piece of work shown in Figure 3.2 on page 38 was done by ten year-old Eleanor, in response to the activity in Figure 3.1 opposite. Eleanor evaluated this activity as 'better than our usual book reviews'. In fact according to the teacher some 'stunning' work was produced by most pupils in the class.

Before leaving this section, try to reflect on the following questions either individually or in a year group meeting:

Questions

- When was I last being 'creative' in my lesson planning?

- How flexible am I in meeting the learning needs of the able children?

- Does teaching facts and skills take up most of my teaching time?

- Do I ascertain whether my most able pupils don't already know what I am going to teach them?

- How much individual construction of knowledge is being engaged in by my most able pupils?

A 'crystal ball' sequel

Have you ever wished when you have finished a book that there was more? Have you wished that you could find out what happened to the characters afterwards?

You might have hoped that the author would write a sequel. What is a sequel? A sequel is a book which continues the story begun by the original book.

How do people go about writing a sequel to a novel?

- *First of all they have to use their imagination to see the character's futures, rather like looking into a crystal ball.*

- *They must, of course, know the original story extremely well.*

NOW Just dream for a moment. The publisher of your favourite book has asked you to write a sequel to it.

It would be helpful to think about the style the book is written in: Does the author use long or short sentences? What kind of descriptive techniques are used? Does s/he tend to be humorous or sad?

Begin by planning the story line. Think about how you will attract the same kind of readers as those who bought the original book. The number of chapters and other decisions about the structure of the book need to be made. The publisher would like you to send in at least one sample chapter with some smartly presented outline ideas for the rest of the book.

Of course, you may want to send the publisher the whole manuscript!

Figure 3.1 A 'crystal ball' sequel activity (from *Bright Challenge*, Casey and Koshy, 1995)

Wuthering Heights
The sequel

I came back to Wuthering Heights I don't know why, but I felt I had left without saying goodbye. When news reached me of Heathcliff's death, I left immediately so not to see the upset faces of Catherine and Edgar, hopefully Cathy had forgiven Heathcliff of all wrong. But I have to admit I did go there really to see Nelly who I still love deep in my heart.

When I finally got to the fields I went straight to where Nelly lived before I departed . I knocked at the door expecting an elderly woman the same age as I. The door creaked and to my surprise there stood the spitting image of my dear Nelly. To fill you in of my last years, I am a retired doctor, not saying that I disliked being one but that I am becoming old and weary and still a bachelor.

" Who be you, and what be you wanting?" the young lady asked suspiciously. Then I realised she must be Nelly's daughter ...

by Eleanor

Figure 3.2   A sequel to *Wuthering Heights* by Eleanor, aged 10

Interacting with peer groups

A dilemma often experienced by those who strive to offer our most able pupils the best possible ways of fulfilling their potential, is with regard to their relationships with peer groups. What do we mean by this? Many higher ability pupils who show remarkable academic talent can often be matched with those several years older. They could easily cope with the content from a higher level in the National Curriculum. So what should be done?

One solution often considered is moving them up to a class where the pupils may be a few years older. This needs to be carefully considered. A higher ability pupil may not have the same emotional maturity as older pupils. Those parents who fear that social interaction may not take place for their children in a higher class may decide to keep the child with the same age group. This may raise another complex problem in that often these pupils need opportunities to have interactions with pupils at a similar intellectual level. Grouping the most able pupils for projects or activities within the school from different classes may offer one possible solution. Some organisations which support the education of very able children (a list of contacts are provided at the end of the book) offer enrichment programmes on weekends and holidays. The level of challenge and advanced concepts offered in some of these classes has been found to be impressive.

The teacher's role in meeting the needs of higher ability pupils

Lists of characteristics for identifying pupils of higher ability are widely available. What about a set of characteristics to consider the features of the 'best' teacher for meeting the needs of the able child? Take a little time out and make a list of what you need to do to become that special kind of teacher. Does your list include some of the following?

- Accept that my pupils may know more than I do.

- Knowing the solution is not a prerequisite for beginning an exploration. It is OK for me to take a shared role with my pupils to arrive at a satisfactory conclusion.

- Understand that I may need to seek outside help for certain subjects or topics for some of my pupils if they show exceptional talents in certain areas.

- Appreciate the need to ask challenging questions, which encourages curiosity and creative thinking.

- Be flexible in my teaching style when I deal with high ability pupils. I need to accept that the pace and quality of the lesson may have to be different for the very able pupils.

- I may need to set up special groupings for different subject areas and for special interest topics in order to facilitate opportunities for sharing complex ideas amongst pupils of similar ability.

- I need to include higher ability pupils among those who need praise and encouragement from me.

Classroom environment

A stimulating classroom environment plays an important part in effective provision for higher ability pupils. Suitable resources need to be provided for able children to be engaged in curiosity pursuits. Observation of very able pupils in their classroom settings have convinced us that resources such as logic puzzles, details of external competitions and Information Technology facilities make a real difference in the provision for higher ability pupils. In some schools we have seen special areas being set up for higher ability pupils to be engaged in enrichment projects. Quite often we have seen pupils spending substantial amounts of time in these mini-enrichment centres working on challenging projects, alone or with specialist teachers, adult mentors or older pupils.

Summary

In this chapter we have considered some of the special needs of higher ability pupils. These needs include their social, emotional and cognitive requirements. We have shared some of our experiences – both exciting and sad – of spending time with these pupils. We have made some suggestions as to how some of their special needs can be met. We have tried to highlight the need for teachers of these pupils to consider their own possible strengths and weaknesses with regard to the provision for higher ability pupils.

4

A Square Deal for Able and Exceptionally Able Pupils

In Chapter 3 we focused on some of the special needs of higher ability pupils. Some discussion of their learning needs also took place. Adopting strategies to enable you to make appropriate provision for able pupils through the curriculum, is, we think, one of the most challenging tasks facing a teacher. During the in-service courses we run, the sessions specifically dealing with curriculum differentiation strategies targeting the most able pupils have always brought the most exciting responses. In this chapter we look specifically at some of the strategies which have been found to be most practical and useful by the teachers we have worked with. We have included many examples of how teachers have achieved high quality work from their most able pupils, with exemplars of pupils' work to further illustrate the point that with increased awareness and careful planning much can be achieved in all schools.

A reminder

We would like to remind our readers of the complexity in understanding the whole notion of 'higher ability'. We would also like to reiterate our own stance that labelling children as 'gifted', 'not gifted', 'able' or 'not able' is not an effective strategy for classroom provision. This does not mean that we don't believe that exceptional abilities exist or that the needs of the most able can be met by regarding them as a homogeneous group. We believe that by viewing ability as a continuum we can adequately meet the needs of the most able within the classroom, if we use enough flexibility in both identifying pupils' abilities and assessing any area-specific aptitudes. Howard Gardner's Multiple Intelligences theory certainly offers us a practical way to think about children's diverse talents.

The CK model

When starting to think about effective classroom provision for higher ability pupils we often use our 'CK Square Deal' model, as shown in Figure 4.1, as a framework for discussion. We can offer an overview of our perceptions of how this model may provide an effective, practical way of thinking about educating our able children. After setting the issue of provision within the 'Square Deal' model we will expand on issues which arise from the model.

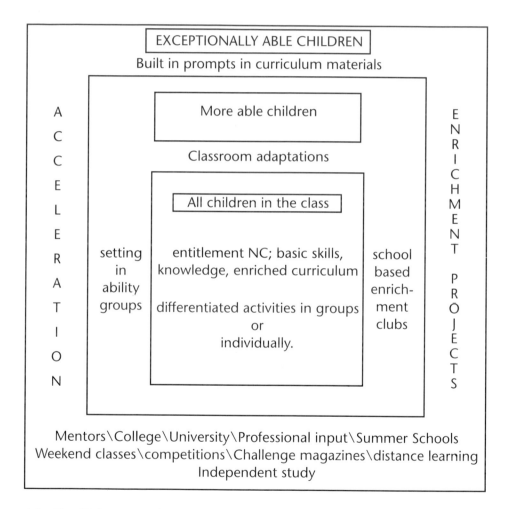

Figure 4.1 The CK Square Deal model for able and exceptionally able children

As the strategies for curriculum provision suggested in the 'Square Deal' model assume some familiarity with terms often used in the context of educating the most able, we will briefly introduce them here. Three such terms which are associated with effective provision through the curriculum are:

- differentiation

- enrichment

- acceleration

They will now be briefly interpreted.

Differentiation

Curriculum differentiation is a term used to signify how a teacher tries to match learning to pupils' ability, aptitudes and learning style. The two ways in which this is practised in classrooms are:

- differentiation by task

- differentiation by outcome

An example of differentiation by task is when a teacher gives one group of pupils addition operations giving totals up to 20 and giving another group addition sums with totals up to 10, because she knows that the latter group can only deal with smaller numbers.

The second, differentiation by outcome, is more open-ended and is likely to be more effective in providing a challenging task to a group of higher ability pupils who have mastered addition of numbers very well. They are unlikely to need to practise the same skills, and an excess of repetition may turn them off mathematics. An example of this was seen in a Year 3 classroom when the teacher put the following on the board:

The answer is 24
What are the questions?

and asked her pupils to contribute the best and most interesting ways of arriving at the answer 24. The responses were collected at the end of the lesson in a plenary discussion, and the most able group was asked to organise a display of what had been done. Figure 4.2 on page 44 shows what was included in that display, and speaks for itself in terms of how the challenge was met by the pupils.

Enrichment

In the process of enrichment, the teacher plans the learning experiences with opportunities built in for broadening the concepts. An enrichment style of learning is likely to be more exciting and qualitatively superior than mere repetition of

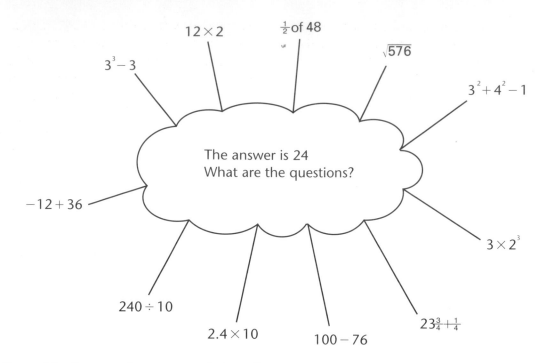

Figure 4.2 Responses to an open-ended question

concepts or just learning more facts and skills. A well-designed enrichment project can open up new realms of learning for the pupils and can be more intellectually satisfying. An enrichment project which involves children in creating a new counting system may lead them on to researching other number systems, as well as deepening their understanding of our own number system. Such projects are useful for all children and the most able pupils, in our experience, may get involved in some complex enquiries through this project. It is worth remembering that enrichment can, of course, lead to differentiation by outcome.

Acceleration

This term often produces more confusion among teachers than the previous two. At its simplest level, we interpret it as pupils being able to move to higher levels of learning of the content in a linear fashion. In terms of the National Curriculum, a Year 5 child doing the work which draws on the content from level 7 or 8 of the National Curriculum can be said to be subject to accelerated content. Early examination entry is a resulting possibility. The term 'accelerated' is also used by many to mean that the child has been moved up by two or three years. Here too, the process of 'acceleration' may lead to that pupil being entered for examinations at an earlier age than is normally expected.

The newspapers often tell us of 10 and 11 year-old children doing GCSE and A Level mathematics, and we would like to digress a moment and share a question which often puzzles us: why is it that most of the accelerated examination entries we read about are in mathematics? We have speculated about many reasons, but would like to leave you to suggest your own explanations for the above question.

Now back to the CK model. As can be seen in Figure 4.1 on page 42, the starting point of effective provision for able children is the classroom. It is based on a whole school approach and is set firmly in the context of the National Curriculum. The whole model is built on the basis that a rich curriculum should be available for all pupils. The aim is to provide stimulation to further develop the aptitudes and specific talents of the higher ability pupils by modifying, differentiating and enriching the basic curriculum as the need arises. The reliance on the class teacher in this model is very high. He or she will work in partnership with the child's parents and draw on the expertise of other agencies as well as the broader community.

The basic curriculum entitlement

So, as the inner square of the CK model suggests, good quality learning experiences are provided in all subjects for all pupils. Most of the activities will be set within the structure of the National Curriculum, which is a basic entitlement for all pupils. It is and always has been devised as the 'minimum entitlement', but we strongly believe that before considering extensions and enrichment programmes we need to ensure that pupils do have a strong knowledge base. Any advanced learning programmes built on a resilient structure of knowledge of facts and skills are likely to be more effective. We know of many pupils who have outstanding potential for learning very advanced concepts and who are also very creative, but who are handicapped by their lack of knowledge of number operations, multiplication tables, spellings and so on. Within the classroom situation, through discussions, questioning and effective differentiation of the curriculum, to some extent the needs of the very able will also be met. Having enriched classroom experiences also creates an environment for all pupils to do their best and provides the teacher and others who are involved in teaching the pupils with opportunities to identify higher ability pupils. Conferences with parents, test results, self-assessment by pupils, portfolios and Records of Achievement will also provide information for teachers to consider special provision.

Providing for 'more able' children

When the whole class is being provided with learning experiences based on the National Curriculum in an appropriately differentiated style, it should be possible for an observant teacher to identify the pupils who may need opportunities for more advanced work. This may be in a single curriculum area or in areas of individual interest, which may not be directly related to the National Curriculum content. In these circumstances you may consider 'setting' for subjects where pupils will get an opportunity to work and communicate with peers of similar ability, so that they may be challenged and stimulated by each other. It may be that the extra provision will take the form of enrichment projects or it may happen within the structure of 'interest' related clusters. The content of what is included in school-based enrichment programmes may have a National Curriculum starting point, providing more time for adult and peer interaction or research. These programmes may be followed within the classroom, in year groups or in enrichment clusters within the school. We also know of enrichment projects being shared by pupils of several schools in the same locality.

The decision as to whether children work in groups or individually will be dependent on the nature of the interest and the learning style of the individual pupil. For example, if several pupils are interested in film-making, a group working on a project to actually produce a film seems sensible, whereas a child who shows a strong passion to find out more about an aspect of Victorian life (after having learned about it in a lesson) may be set an individual project to produce something which is intellectually satisfying, such as putting up a display and making a presentation to the class or school.

A word of caution should be included here concerning what we think are the adverse effects of badly planned and organised 'setting' or 'projects'. While at its best we have seen some of the most creative and outstanding work produced in 'sets' and in project groups, more disturbingly we have also witnessed some pupils being subjected to more 'drill' and doing more of the same within groupings of higher ability pupils. The latter, we think, may do more harm than good.

Where extra provision has been organised, both the parents of the children in your school and the wider community can make significant contributions.

The exceptionally able pupils

Who are 'exceptionally able' pupils? HMI (1992, p. 1) refers to these children as those who perform years ahead of their peer group. In terms of their IQ they may show high potential. It may be that they will display outstanding abilities in one or more subject areas – perhaps music, language or mathematics. We are often told those pupils who have exceptional abilities are quite often effectively identified by both their parents and teachers. This seems true even in the case of some of the parents we've met who don't believe that because of their background of disadvantage and deprivation their children could be 'so gifted'! We have experience of working with a six year-old daughter of a lorry driver who said:

When she started reading shop signs and words on shopping packages at the age of two, we thought she was picking these up from our conversations. But when she started reading fluently at three, it was a shock because I myself can't read that much and we are very poor. You just don't expect this from our sort of background.

Amazing talents of all kinds are often identified by parents very early in a child's life, although sometimes talents do go unnoticed if proper attention is not given. Within a family where parents have to leave their children with other people for most of the day in order to earn a living or where a child who belongs to a family where no one talks to him or her, or where there are no books to read, it may well be that talents may go unrecognised.

Exceptionally able children – whether their special ability is in a single area or is of the all-rounders type – may need further support within the framework of the school setting. One of the strategies may be to set them work from a higher level of the National Curriculum for part of the time. If you look at a class timetable, it can be seen that for a large part of the time pupils are given experiences in a variety of things. School assemblies, games, swimming, drama and music all play a part in children's development. One of the positive features of the National Curriculum is that all pupils now have an opportunity to experience a broad and balanced curriculum. If a child shows outstanding ability in some aspect, acceleration of content within the National Curriculum is one effective strategy to be adopted.

It may be that exceptionally able pupils can spend some time with older children for some parts of the National Curriculum based lessons. The strategy of moving the pupil up by one or two years has also proved successful in some cases. Here the decision must take several factors into account – physical size, emotional maturity, physical co-ordination being some of them. We know of a four year-old who could hardly write his name but who could wordprocess some outstanding pieces of work, and of six year-olds being able to display very high levels of mathematical knowledge, but who were unable to record their work clearly because of the lack of experience of recording skills. Both accelerating in content areas and moving children up are often suggested as the simplest of options. However, these options need very careful thought.

Very rarely have we come across large numbers of exceptionally able pupils in one class whose needs cannot fully be met within the school. But there have been occasions when these pupils have shown the need to have personal mentors. There are instances in history of people who eventually made major intellectual contributions – John Stuart Mill and Bertrand Russell for example – who learnt a great deal from their personal mentors. It may be that some of your exceptionally able pupils need more resources to pursue their complex and advanced interests.

Weekend programmes, made available by organisations which support higher ability pupils, are worth considering. The teacher may also need to counsel these pupils. We know cases of exceptionally able pupils who 'long' to talk to some one who 'understands' the loneliness of having to live with interests which don't 'fit into' their peer group interests. It may be that they have thought of some ideas in physics which need a 'specialist' listener. Their talents needs to be recognised and celebrated.

Special programmes run by adults who are aware of the needs of these pupils – both at a personal and cognitive level – can be a great support to these pupils. These programmes may offer these pupils the assurance that there is nothing 'wrong' with them for having unusual interests and that their special gifts are highly valued. Teachers need to have a list of the types of programmes available for these pupils. Some information about agencies who provide special programmes is given at the end of this book. It is also useful to have a noticeboard in school where details of local and national competitions are displayed.

No two children's needs are ever exactly alike. This makes provision for exceptionally able pupils particularly challenging. Having all the exceptionally able pupils sent to one school has been suggested as an option by certain groups of people. We leave teachers to consider the merits or disadvantages of such a strategy. Reading this book and reflecting on what has been put forward by us will, hopefully, prepare you to make the most informed decisions.

Curriculum provision for the most able

In the following sections we will provide examples of some effective strategies employed by teachers to encourage their higher ability pupils to produce high quality work.

Offering creative opportunities

In Chapter 3 we briefly discussed the importance of encouraging creativity in the classroom. Teachers have often told us about their difficulty in trying to be 'creative' when demands on their time – especially after the introduction of the National Curriculum – have become greater. But through reflecting on the role of creativity they become persuaded to rethink their practices. So where did they start?

The first step in encouraging children to be 'creative' is to look at some of the activities you already do. Given the opportunity, all children are capable of being more creative, but in our experience the more able pupils are capable of producing some very imaginative pieces of work. Gardner (1995, p. 15) talks about his Boston project where pupils were asked to take a chance with their routine book reviews, and the results were extremely pleasing. The following examples are selected to show you that often only a little effort is needed to make yourself look at the activities you regularly give children to do and to modify and extend them. In Chapter 3 we provided the example of pupils being asked to write the first chapter of a sequel to their favourite book, where some of the most 'reluctant' writers produced excellent pieces of work.

Similarly, a Year 9 teacher asked her top mathematics group to write a few pages on how to teach probability, as if they were writing a text book for Year 6 pupils. The results were so outstanding that a group of pupils were entrusted with the task of producing a user-friendly mathematics booklet of 'their probability pages' using a desk-top package, thus providing another opportunity for pupils to be creative in their IT lessons.

Another example of a normal classroom activity being modified was provided by a Year 4 teacher in a dictionary-work lesson. Pupils were asked to find alternate meanings of some given words and the results are shown in Figure 4.3 on page 50.

Referring to the work produced by the pupils, the teacher observed:

Nearly every time I set dictionary work – after all learning dictionary skills is an important part of language education – my children groan and moan. They were asked to work on the 'word-treasure' activity with two other children and I have not seen so much excitement in my class for a very long time in any lesson; let alone in a dictionary lesson. The idea of having to come up with humorous options made them laugh at everything and at themselves, a good therapy. They analysed words, made up meanings and looked up correct meanings of words in their dictionaries. Now I use this idea in the context of the class topic. I have a permanent display of options of words in my classroom and along the corridor and you can often hear other pupils reading the words, choosing the correct options and having a laugh at some of the 'daft meanings'.

Take a few minutes to look at your planning records and think about how you might 'change' some of the activities you do regularly to include more exciting and creative ideas. Excitement in learning something can very often lead to better efforts and higher quality work. Many teachers have told us that by providing creative opportunities it is not just the quality of the work which is enhanced; the inspiration resulting from a new way of looking at things has often encouraged some 'lazy' able pupils to produce 'more' written work.

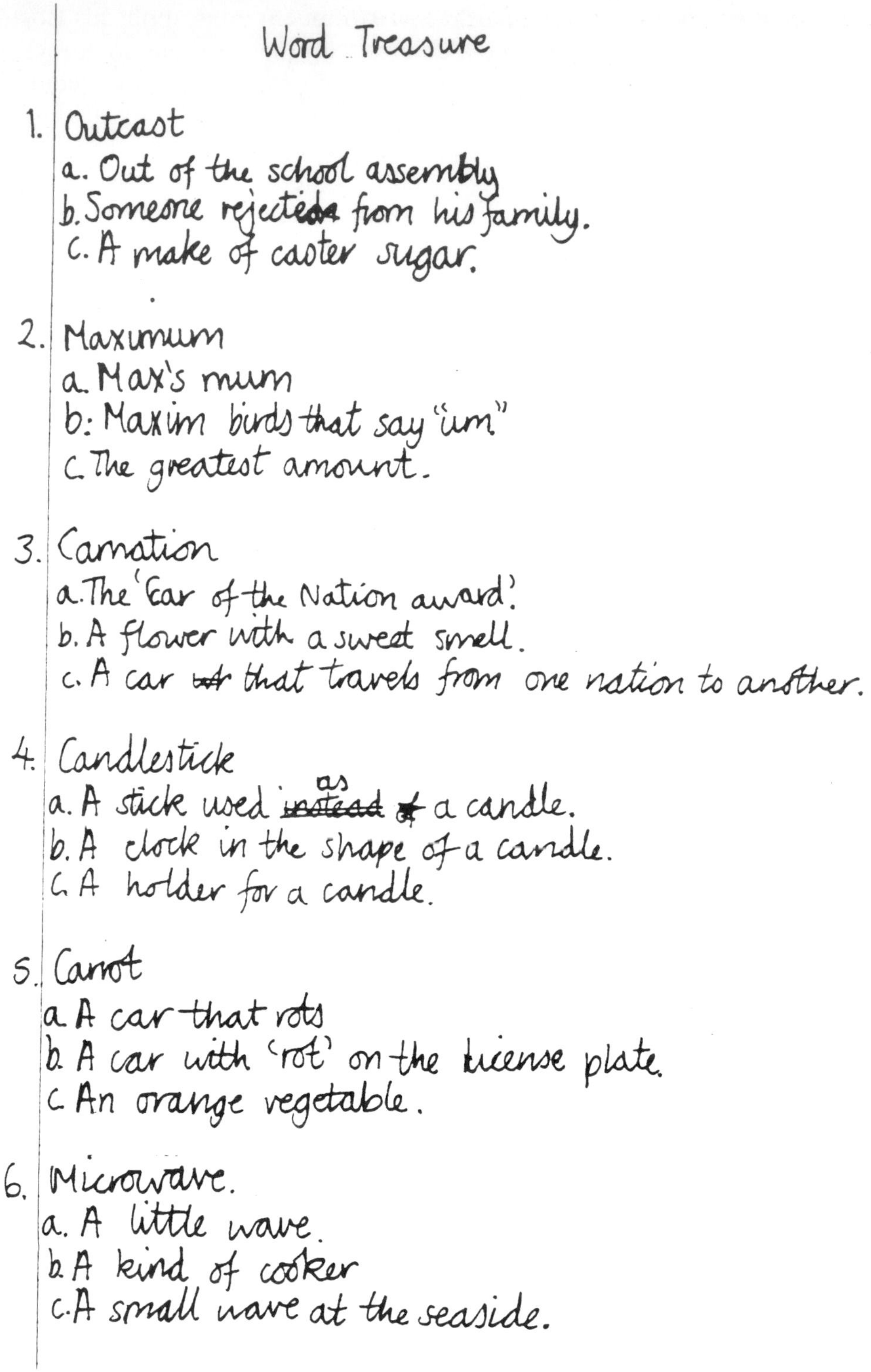

Word Treasure

1. Outcast
   a. Out of the school assembly
   b. Someone rejected from his family.
   c. A make of caster sugar.

2. Maximum
   a. Max's mum
   b: Maxim birds that say "um"
   c. The greatest amount.

3. Carnation
   a. The 'Ear of the Nation award'.
   b. A flower with a sweet smell.
   c. A car that travels from one nation to another.

4. Candlestick
   a. A stick used instead of a candle.
   b. A clock in the shape of a candle.
   c. A holder for a candle.

5. Carrot
   a. A car that rots
   b. A car with 'rot' on the license plate.
   c. An orange vegetable.

6. Microwave.
   a. A little wave.
   b. A kind of cooker
   c. A small wave at the seaside.

Figure 4.3 Example of modified dictionary work

Encourage lively and variable presentations

In our dealings with very able pupils we have often witnessed a 'reluctance' to be engaged in routine tasks. In many cases we have felt their unwillingness to do the 'same' type of work again and again was quite justifiable. A practical suggestion is to offer pupils variety in the presentation of their work after they have conducted their enquiries and research. The following ideas may explain what we mean:

- Arrange a role play showing 'good' and 'bad' leaders for the class and ask a group of children to draw up a poster showing their 'ideal leader' highlighting what qualities make a good leader. Display and present their poster to other groups of pupils. Extend the study to comparing their finding and results to both local, national and international leaders

- Ask the children to write their version of a school brochure for prospective pupils using selected mediums for effective presentation

- Set the question: If you were in charge of your school for one day and moved into the headteacher's office, write a diary of what your day had been like

- Encourage the pupils to create a school anthem

- Encourage reflective writing by asking the children to write an account of how other children may describe them

- Develop pupils' interpersonal skills and communication expertise by asking them to interview a selected sample of adults on their feelings about mathematics and, based on the data collected, make a three-minute presentation using posters, charts and so on. Then make a list of what a teacher can do to make his or her pupils 'like' mathematics

- Write and present a radio play on a selected theme or book

- Design a new animal and evaluate what advice you would need to give the British Zoo authorities for them to consider keeping it there

Ask questions which demand higher levels of thinking

In Chapter 3 we presented some interesting questions which used the 'would you rather . . .' style. One of the most fruitful strategies to encourage thinking and problem solving is to adopt the kind of questioning which raises children's curiosity and makes them search for original responses. We often find that higher ability pupils often respond very well to questions which contain:

- What if . . . ?

- What will I do . . . ?

- Why is . . . ?

HUMPTY DUMPTY

- *What if they put him together incorrectly?*

- *What could Humpty see from the top of the wall?*

- *Why is Humpty on the wall?*

- *Should Humpty be on the wall?*

- *If Humpty Dumpty came to your school how would you treat him?*

- *Can you think of ways to repair Humpty?*

- *Can you draw Humpty Dumpty on the computer screen? (Using a painting program – Information Technology)*

- *How could you put Humpty back on the wall?*

Figure 4.4 Generating discussion with very young children

- Can you think of a different . . . ?

- How . . . ?

The ideas in Figure 4.4 were used by a nursery class teacher to generate some exciting discussions.

Another instance was during one Christmas period when all the teachers in a primary school decided to ask their children to:

- rewrite the part of the Christmas story involving the Three Kings, changing it to include a fourth king or

- write a diary of the fourth king

Most of the very able pupils' responses were reported to be highly 'original', with every pupil having created a worthwhile product. The excitement was considerable and included one entry from a six year-old who described the fourth king taking 'a bowl of water from the river Thames' as his gift to Baby Jesus. We studied the samples of work from different age groups. Perhaps the most remarkable thing was that although there were differences in writing skills, in terms of quality of thinking and imaginative ideas some very young children did equally well or sometimes better than the older ones. There is something for us to think about here!

Reflecting on questions which encourage creative thinking at the time of planning a class topic is good practice. Questions generated in the planning sessions can be stored away in an 'ideas' book or file.

Encourage higher levels of thinking

All children need to be encouraged to engage in higher levels of thinking. Some of the strategies suggested in the earlier sections of this chapter will undoubtedly help the teacher to evaluate the quality of the questions they ask.

A theoretical model which many teachers found to be a very useful framework for curriculum planning is based on Bloom's Taxonomy (1956). The cognitive domain of Bloom's Taxonomy of objectives is used internationally to consider how curriculum planning can take into account the six levels of thinking, leading to effective differentiation of the curriculum and the design of sound enrichment activities.

In the following sections we present an account of the six levels of thinking, with our interpretations of what each level entails. We then provide examples of how teachers of different key stages have incorporated these principles to give their pupils access to higher levels of thinking.

Bloom's Taxonomy

Bloom's Taxonomy is based on cognitive abilities and proposed six levels of thinking. They are:

Knowledge
Comprehension
Application   higher levels
Analysis
Synthesis
Evaluation

One way to consider these levels for the purpose of curriculum planning is to view them as levels of thinking making increasing demands on the cognitive processes of the pupils. Activities which incorporate higher levels of thinking are shown to be very suitable for the most able pupils. Now we turn to an explanation of each level.

Knowledge

This level is concerned with the acquisition of knowledge – learning facts, for example. This is the basic level which asks the learner to identify, list and describe newly-acquired knowledge. This may involve some repetition for some pupils. Higher ability pupils may already have a good knowledge base. If not, they must acquire the skills to find out facts when they need them. Facts may be remembered quite easily, even though the remembering is not always accompanied by understanding of concepts related to them. Spelling of words, mathematical symbols, terminology and names of scientific equipment can be classified under this category.

Comprehension

This level is concerned with showing what knowledge has been acquired and trying to explain what has been learnt. Paraphrasing what has been learnt, answering questions based on a passage which has been read, or summarising what is read may be the type of suitable activity at this level. In a normal classroom situation, comprehension exercises which ask direct questions or mathematics word-problems based on a suggested algorithm or number operation are examples of work at this level.

Application

At this level pupils can be asked to make use of what they have learnt and apply their knowledge in practical and problem-solving situations. This level requires a higher level of demand on their cognitive processing and higher ability pupils are often capable of taking problem tasks to complex levels. Children involved in problem-solving activities in technology, mathematics or science need to apply concepts in order to solve problems.

The next three levels are often referred to as the higher levels of thinking:

Analysis

Analysis is a more complex skill, which involves looking at situations and breaking them down into component parts and perceiving relationships between them. Categorising information and seeing patterns and themes emerge are analytical processes. Analysis is very useful for understanding new ideas and making strong connections between ideas. It is a more 'active' process than the first three levels and can result in both discoveries and generalisations.

Synthesis

We often refer to this level as the most 'creative' level. It involves looking at things in a different way, asking the question 'what if . . .', 'hypothesise' or 're-create'. This level fosters a thinking style which is more original or unexpected, and encourages taking risks and creating new ideas. Our experience suggests that higher ability pupils often take up the challenge of designing something unusual and new very positively. Examples of some 'creative' products were presented earlier in this chapter. A 'would you rather be a bird or a butterfly?' type of question, or being asked to design a new animal, may lead to this level of thinking. Planning activities at this level may take a bit more effort on the teacher's part because they are not easily transportable from textbooks. But when teachers have made the effort they have found the experience and the products of their children's work extremely rewarding.

Evaluation

It is not surprising that this is classified as the highest level of thinking, as it involves many processes – personal reflection, assessment skills, making decisions and appraising the effects of something. Evaluating the effectiveness of personal and others' products of thinking require this type of mental activity. Presentation of projects to others, reviewing one's own and other people's ideas, keeping reflective diaries of events are examples of this type of thinking being encouraged in the classroom.

Although the latter three levels are described as being 'higher levels' of thinking, do not assume that all planning should include all levels. We can certainly share with you our experience that teachers who plan with these levels in mind do find differentiation much easier. They say that even when all the planned ideas are not used in the lessons, thinking about the levels often helps them to challenge the teacher too. The work set at higher levels of thinking makes suitable enrichment projects, as it encourages enquiry and the search for more knowledge and understanding of a topic.

Curriculum planning examples based on Bloom's Taxonomy

The following sections describe how teachers have used Bloom's Taxonomy as a framework in their planning of classroom topics, subject-related activities and enrichment projects.

Planning of a project on 'weather'

As can be seen on Table 4.1 in this plan, ideas of increasing levels of complexity are introduced.

LEVELS	EXAMPLES
Knowledge	What do you know about weather? What do the following words – rain, hail, rainbow, forecast, snow, storm and so on – mean? Can you collect more weather words and make up a list of what they mean? Make a weather chart using cut out pictures from newspapers for monitoring daily weather
Comprehension	How does it rain? What is the difference between rain and sleet? Can you describe the equipment we use for measuring weather conditions? What would you do to make ice from water? How accurate is the weather forecast in newspapers?
Application	Make a list of things you do in different kinds of weather? What sports are played in different weather conditions? With the help of diagrams explain how rain is formed How do weather conditions differ in different countries?
Analysis	Make up a crossword on weather using the most number of clues Can you explain how each type of weather affects life on earth? Would you rather be a snowflake or a raindrop?
Synthesis	If you could have your 'ideal' weather what would you like? Pretend you are a raindrop; write a biography of a raindrop What would happen if it never rained again?
Evaluation	After learning about weather in the last few weeks which facts have you learnt? What has been the most remarkable? What do you know now that you did not know when we started? When it is snowing, who is likely to say 'This is terrible weather' or 'This is brilliant'? Give reasons

Table 4.1 Example of curriculum planning based on Bloom's Taxonomy

Having a list of questions and ideas on your planning sheet does help effective differentiation, although it is the teacher who has to make the decision on which particular ideas and activities to choose for different groups of children. For example, you may find that some children know quite a lot about 'weather' words and what they all mean; in this case they could be asked to write a biography of a raindrop – an activity listed in the table as involving higher levels of thinking. The following examples are from the work produced by two Key Stage 2 pupils from different schools. Their teachers told us that a good deal of referencing and facts checking occurred during the writing process. The difference in this case was that the knowledge acquired was learnt for a purpose. We were told that if the questions from the first levels only were given to both these pupils they would not have enjoyed the work as much as they did, especially writing a biography of the raindrop. Both Jay and Alfred had always shown great interest in scientific ideas and their work in Figures 4.5 and 4.6 on pages 60 and 61 bears testimony to a differentiated idea being used successfully by their respective class teachers.

The weather crossword shown in Figure 4.7 on page 62 is another example of an able group being given a task from the 'analysis' level. Again, the research they had conducted to design a crossword was described to be 'tremendous' and the amount of checking and preparation happened because they were given a challenge which was both interesting and interactive. The two teachers also told us that the group who worked on the weather crossword did not always enjoy routine activities of answering questions.

An enrichment project on 'codes' in a secondary (Year 7) class

This example shows how Bloom's Taxonomy was used by a secondary school to design an enrichment project on codes. The work was planned to take place during enrichment project time made available to pupils within school hours, although much of the work was also taken home by pupils. The project was one of a number pupils could choose from and the group was expected to put displays up at the end of six weeks. All pupils were free to choose 'codes' as their project and, through careful planning, the teacher was able to guide the pupils by providing them with tasks of increasing complexity and challenge. Here is the plan:

The code project

Knowledge

- What is the difference between a code and a cipher?
- What does cryptography mean?
- Find out as many different types of codes as you can and illustrate them
- What are postcodes?
- What does a forensic scientist do?

Comprehension

- Make a chart of famous codes and show how each category of codes fits into the chart
- Where do you find bar codes? How do they work?
- Collect some historic codes and explain when and how they were used
- What is a periodic table? Write out what 12 of the symbols mean

Application

- Make up a code for your friend
- Make up an advertisement to invite people to ask for assistance from a cryptologist
- Investigate what difference it makes to the delivery of a first class letter whether it is sent with or without a postcode
- Write a story which uses codes and ciphers to solve a mystery or a detective story

Analysis

- Why do some people call a code a pattern?
- Make a collection of different codes and list the different strategies used for decoding them
- What do you prefer, a code or a cipher? Give your reasons
- What is genetic code? Explain an original use for it

Synthesis

- Invent a code and use it for all communications for a day, including communication to the teacher

- What is a trademark? Can you make one up?

- Design a code machine and explain how it may work

Evaluation

- Write an account with the title 'The day when all the codes disappeared'

- Of all the ways we use codes today, which one do you think is the most efficient? Explain your reasons

We saw a stunning exhibition resulting from the work on codes, in the school where the above planning took place. Teachers commented on the high level of interest and motivation of all the pupils who took part in the project. Some higher ability pupils took weeks to complete the assignments and the results were outstanding. Interest-based enrichment projects are increasingly being introduced in many schools. These projects also provide opportunities for meaningful and interesting homework, which is less likely to be viewed as a 'chore'.

It is now time for you to do a little planning yourself. Either with a colleague or by yourself, make a plan showing how you would take Bloom's levels of thinking into account when planning to teach your current topic. Then make a list of which pupils in your class may be given the different tasks you have included in your plan.

Although the examples of planning based on Bloom's Taxonomy are related to general topics, the same principles can be applied to specific curriculum areas. Some examples of these are given in the next chapter. Finally, give yourself a challenge. Think of all the lessons you have taught in the last three days. Make a note of the activities from your plan, to see which of them could be described as belonging to Bloom's higher levels of thinking. Experience has shown us that a great deal of the work that goes on in classrooms are only targeting the first three levels. The National Curriculum deals with the first three levels to support children's acquisition of basic skills and knowledge. It is up to the teacher to enrich the curriculum by employing some of the strategies we have suggested. The result, we can assure you, will be satisfying for both your children and yourself.

THE BIOGRAPHY OF A RAINDROP

Introduction:

A raindrop is evaporated salt water (without the sodium chloride) which has reformed into water again by the weight of the steam (cloud) which cause it to turn back to water. The salt water, when evaporated leaves the salt behind because salt water is a solution and not chemically bonded like methane or benzene and can easily be separated by heating it. That is the reason for rain, it does not just come from any old place, it comes from the sea.

Here is a story about a drop of sea water, which finds out what it is like to be a raindrop with a pretty intelligent friend:

Once upon a time, there was a little raindrop called Dick. He had lots and lots of friends because he lived in the Indian Ocean where wildlife was endless and there were vast amounts of little seadrops like him. His best friend was a little seadrop called Harry. He was very interested in physics, chemistry and ecology. He knew about evaporation, but he was curious about one thing: what it was like to be a raindrop.

One fine morning Dick was doing his studies when Harry popped in. He said "what do think it would be like to be a raindrop?" "Well probably quite exciting Harry though I am not all that sure". "Well say, should we try it out then?" "Oh! no it could be dangerous we better not!" exclaimed Dick. "Come on, Dick," tempted Harry. "Well, all right but if it is dangerous don't blame me." "O.K." said Harry excitedly. "Let's go to the surface!" "I've got a bad feeling about this!" cried Dick.

"Here we are at the surface. Now we have to wait to get evaporatated . . . everapated . . . evra – oh fiddlesticks!" "I think you mean evaporated," put in Dick. "Yes!, Well donebe, you said it!"

Later on at the surface Harry and Dick were beginning to vapourise into the air. While they were doing so they found they were a lot less salty and began to worry. "I don't feel so good," said Dick. "Nor do I," added Harry. "Whose clever idea was this anyway?" asked Harry. "Yours" put in Dick angrily. "Help!" they both cried as both of them were vapourised into the air.

One day later they were hurled to the ground as raindrops. "Well, Harry you got your wish you are now a raindrop," said Dick. "Look, what's that!," exclaimed Harry, as they passed a rainbow. "I got my wish at last," said Harry. This is wonderful. Wwwwweeeeeeee!" "I feel sick," cried Dick!

THE END

Figure 4.5 Biography of a raindrop by Jay, aged 8

THE BIOGRAPHY OF A RAINDROP

Not so long ago, in the warm, deep Pacific Ocean, there was a water molecule. It couldn't speak, think or move except when a force was exerted upon it. Suddenly, a wave threw it into the air. It landed on a volcanic island with a squillion other water molecules.

The warm soft rock from a VERY recent volcanic eruption evaporated them. As they got more and more excited, the molecules spread further apart and left the salt behind. They were water vapour!

As they rose, they cooled, making a cloud. Small particles of dust, smoke, sulphate and salt known as condensation nuclei pulled the water molecules together into small droplets! The water vapour soon became a large cumulus cloud. Cumulus are white, fluffy clouds. By now there were raindrops in the cloud. As the cloud got bigger it turned into a huge Cumulus congestus, towering into the sky.

One of the raindrops, called Bill, was having a good time. He was talking with his friends and bouncing up and down in the cloud because of the static electricity in the cloud. He went up to the positively charged top of the towering cloud, and down rocketing through it, collecting more and more droplets on his body as he went. He went up and down a lot, until was too heavy to be supported. The fat raindrop Bill fell SMACK into a puddle, and started to swim. After the storm, the sun came out and the puddle heated up. Bill felt hot, and then evaporated, along with the rest of the puddle . . . and the cycle began again!

Figure 4.6 Biography of a raindrop by Alfred, aged 7

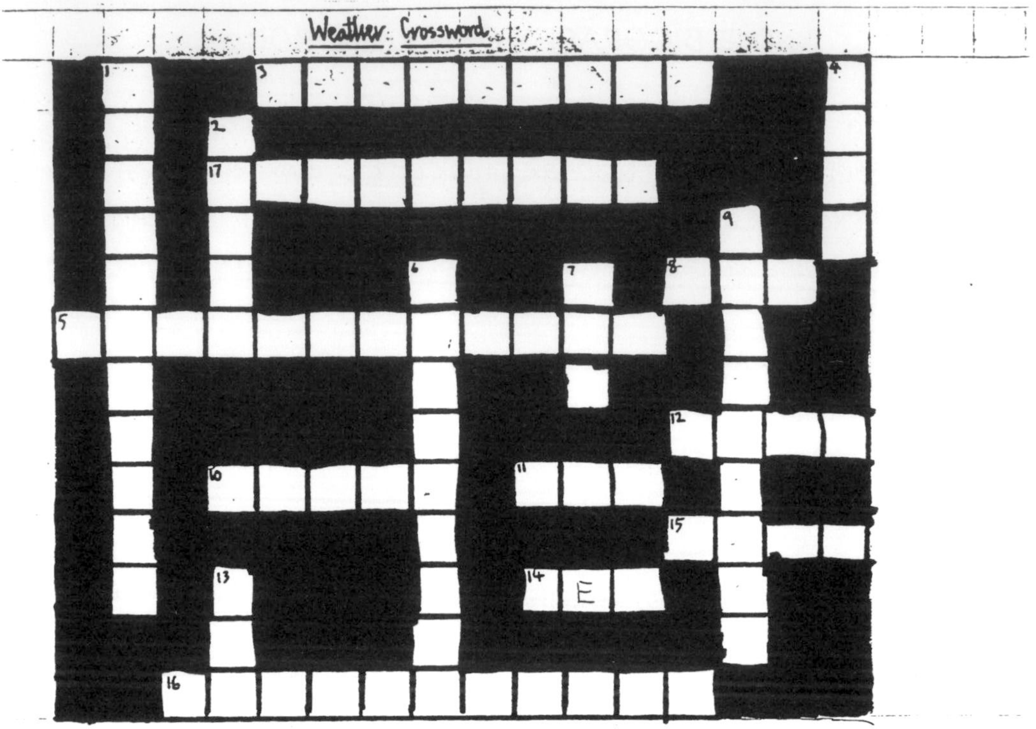

Weather Crossword

Clues across

3 When water turns into a gas.
5 When water drips as the place gets colder.
8 The closest star to the earth.
10 A very strong wind with alot of rain.
11 Some people say as thin as ___.
12 It can blow all sorts of things.
14 When grass gets wet in the morning.
15 Hard rain.
16 How hot or cold something is.
17 It comes before thunder.

Clues down

1 Used to measure how hot or cold the air is.
2 A big white thing that floats in the sky.
4 When you are not hot or cold.
6 Used to measure the air pressure.
7 Similar to mist.
9 Causes alot of damage when it reaches the land.

1 hour 25 min

by Cam Nin Tran

Figure 4.7 A weather crossword by Cam Nin Tran, aged 9

Summary

This chapter has been devoted to a discussion of strategies to make suitable adaptations to the curriculum. Amongst the strategies a framework for differentiation of the curriculum – Bloom's Taxonomy – was suggested. Several examples were provided to show how the ideas suggested are viable and practical for busy people.

CHAPTER 5

Designing Curriculum Materials for Higher Ability Pupils

In this chapter we will try to generate some principles for designing curriculum materials with higher ability pupils in mind. These principles are embedded in our belief that all teachers can successfully design such curriculum materials. However, there are some factors which can support the teacher in this process. They need to exercise their own creativity and develop an understanding of what is meant by higher levels of thinking. Ideas and activities generated or modified should enrich all pupils' learning; they can raise the expectations of both the pupils and the teacher and consequently raise the level of achievement of most pupils.

All our work with teachers and schools has been based on the belief that developing good quality curriculum materials plays an important part in educating higher ability pupils. Our belief is shared by many others working in the field. One well-known and particularly practical working model – The Schoolwide Enrichment model developed by Renzulli in the USA – is used internationally and has been the subject of much research. Renzulli (1994, pages 15–97) describes his Schoolwide Enrichment model as a detailed blueprint for total school improvement which is designed to promote both 'challenging' and 'high-end learning' through an improvement plan whose aim is to provide an 'alternative to what one student called the "drill and kill approach" by offering an enrichment based model that uses "high-end" learning strategies and accelerated content to improve the performance of all pupils.'

Promoting the use of a challenging, stimulating and creative curriculum is therefore one of our primary activities. In the previous chapter we described some strategies for curriculum planning and one theoretical model which offer some principles for effective curriculum differentiation. The next step is to focus on how to translate the differentiated curriculum into activities. How do we achieve this? What are the guiding principles?

In a small-scale research project at Brunel University entitled 'Bright Challenge' (Casey and Koshy, 1995) we designed curriculum materials in an attempt to generate some practical guidelines to be shared with practising teachers. The activities produced by us were trialled by teachers who provided much stimulus to our own thinking about the most effective methods of curriculum design for the most able pupils. Many schools have since adopted the principles of the 'Bright Challenge' project. We would like to share some of our experiences with you in the following sections.

Some guiding principles for designing enriching activities

Using National Curriculum starting points

As we have a National Curriculum which sets out a broad curriculum base, it does make practical sense to look at all the possibilities of setting up enquiries within its context. 'Putting some life back into the body', in Figure 5.1 on page 66, is an example of designing a project with a National Curriculum starting point. Learning about the human body is a topic dealt with in the National Curriculum. Names of organs in the body and their functions are usually dealt with in most classrooms. This provides children with a strong knowledge base. The activity given below can be tackled at different levels by different ability groups.

During the trialling of this activity, one of the teachers in an inner-city school, Barbara, brought the following notes which she collected while her eight year-old pupils were engaged in tackling the project.

This activity I had only intended giving to a group of my bright children. Soon I changed my mind because while the able group was tackling one of the challenges I had set for them most of the others wanted to join in. I decided to let everyone have a go. Two issues emerged. The first one was that from observing the children doing some parts of this activity, I was surprised at their competence in certain areas, some children I wouldn't have rated as 'very able' emerged as very capable. The other was the length of time some of my pupils would spend on a particular part of the activity because they were really enjoying making a book of the human body. Their knowledge about the human body was enhanced through this project. They conducted much research on the various aspects of the human body. The following are from their conversations in groups.

Maria   I need a long word here
Claire   I have got one – Falx Cerebral, means the brain

SCIENCE

Putting some life back into the body

Do you think that colouring books are only for very young children?

Recently, some 19 year old students who are studying to be doctors were surprised to find that their professor had recommended a colouring book to help them to study the human body and how it works.

Did the medical students enjoy it? Not only did they like it, they told us that they had learned a lot from it because it was so much fun.

NOW

Your project is to produce a book about the human body, its organs and their functions, which is good fun to read. The book is for children who can read quite well. You must try to include things for your readers to do, such as puzzles and questionnaires. As well as learning about some of the miraculous ways in which our bodies work, your book should enable its readers to answer questions such as:

- *Is the alimentary canal the oldest part of the Suez Canal in Egypt?*

- *Are the images we see upside down at the back of our eyes? If this is true, then a telescope which makes something in the sky look upside down is really making it the right way up. Is this a riddle?*

- *Why does blood have to keep moving even when we are resting?*

Use reference books to check your facts!

Figure 5.1 A human body enrichment project (from *Bright Challenge*, Casey and Koshy, 1995)

Emma I am writing down the clues before I forget what it all means
Daniel What do you think is the colour of the veins in your head – are they blue?
Emma We can't find it anywhere, we could phone up a doctor and ask?

The 'human brain' had apparently raised much speculation and research. According to Barbara, this was facilitated by the nature of the activity.

The examples of work shown below emerged from the human body project.

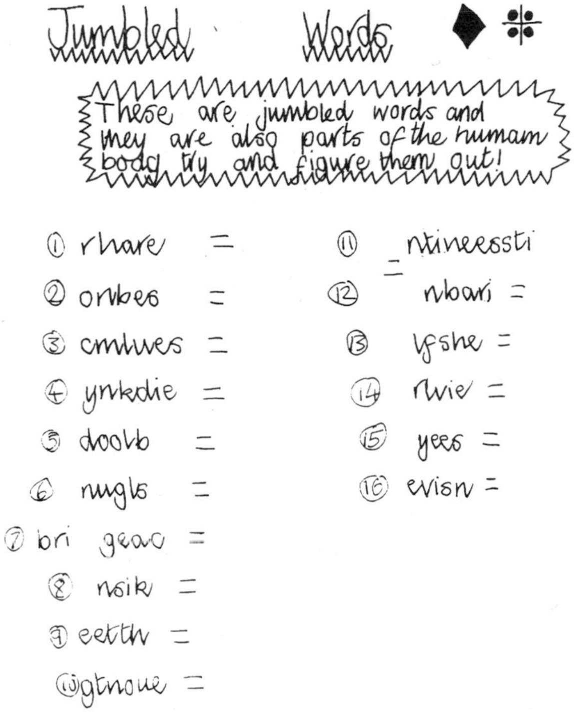
Jumbled Words

These are jumbled words and they are also parts of the human body try and figure them out!

① rhare =
② orbes =
③ cmlues =
④ ynkdie =
⑤ doolb =
⑥ nugls =
⑦ bri geao =
⑧ nsik =
⑨ eetth =
⑩ gtnoue =
⑪ ntineessti =
⑫ nbari =
⑬ fshe =
⑭ rvie =
⑮ yees =
⑯ evisn =

Figure 5.2 Human body anagrams

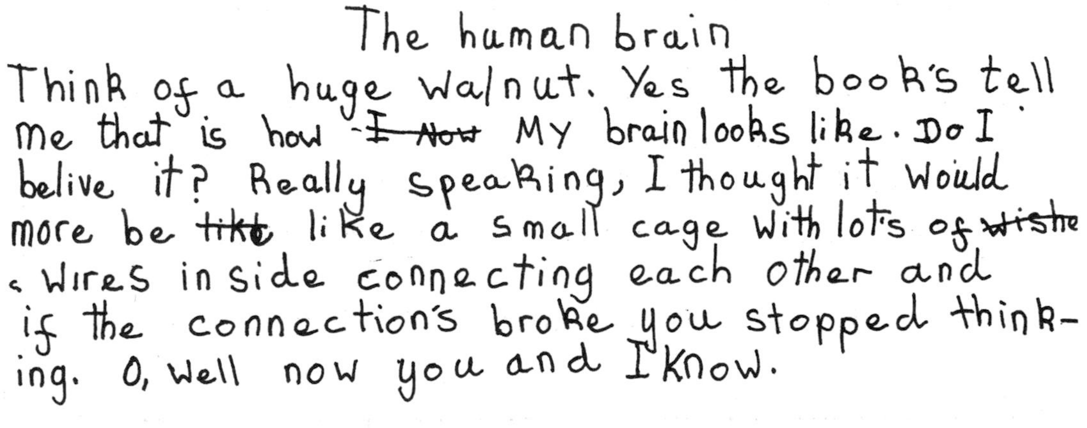
The human brain

Think of a huge walnut. Yes the book's tell me that is how ~~I Now~~ My brain looks like. Do I belive it? Really speaking, I thought it would more be ~~like~~ like a small cage with lot's of ~~wishe~~ wires inside connecting each other and if the connection's broke you stopped thinking. O, well now you and I Know.

Figure 5.3 An extract from a book on the human body by Rishma, aged 8

Using open-ended activities

In striving to offer all the pupils in a class opportunities for fulfilling their potential, the use of open-ended activities can play a very important part. In the following example, a class of Year 4 children was given an investigation to make as many discoveries as they possibly could by looking at how consecutive numbers 'behaved'. Children were given the choice to work by themselves, in pairs or in small groups. They had a week to work on the project and had total freedom to organise work in their free time or break times, or they could take the project home. A presentation was to be made to two Year 4 groups on Friday morning. The class teacher reported that there was much excitement for the project and commented, as Barbara also did, that most of the children in the class could participate in this activity at the level of sophistication they were capable of. Some very able pupils produced some interesting discoveries as can be seen in Figure 5.4 opposite.

Although mathematics investigations of this kind go on in some classrooms as part of Attainment Target 1 – Using and Applying Mathematics – in many schools AT1 is interpreted as closed word problems which are carried out by pupils according to learnt rules.

Using motivating activities

Learning is more effective when you enjoy what you are doing. Setting 'more' complex work for higher ability pupils is a fine strategy as long as the learners' interest is aroused by the work set. We all know that intrinsic motivation is a very powerful contributing factor in the learning process.

As part of a project on 'homes' a group of very able Key Stage 2 children, aged 8, were asked to design their 'dream' home and furnish it with items from an adult catalogue, as long as the total amount they spent did not exceed £1000. The class teacher reported that children showed exceptional interest in this topic which she attributed to the children being given a chance to make decisions. Later, she added that the motivation also arose from having the 'money' to spend. It was very interesting to note the way children were reading big numbers, interpreting money signs, working out prices, doing measurements and being involved in number operations which were usually dealt with in the higher levels of the National Curriculum. Where 'discounts' and 'percentages' were mentioned in the catalogue, on the 'toys' page, children sought clarification at home as to what they meant. One child came to school one morning and taught his peers how to work out percentages on a calculator!

Through the motivation offered by the context, young children were able to access accelerated content as well as being enriched. Many teachers tell us about their

My discoveries so far

1. If you add two consecutive numbers, the answer will always be odd.

2. If you add three consecutive numbers the answer will be even if you start with an odd.

3. You cannot make number 21 by adding four consecutive numbers. I have not tried with five numbers yet. You can with six

$$
\begin{array}{r}
6 \\
7 \\
+\ 8 \\
\hline
21
\end{array}
\qquad
\begin{array}{r}
1 \\
2 \\
3 \\
4 \\
5 \\
+\ 6 \\
\hline
21
\end{array}
$$

4. Say you want to find out which three consecutive numbers add up to 33
divide 33 by 3 $33 \div 3 = 11$
then add the numbers
before and after 11 to 11
$10 + (11) + 12 = 33$

5. Same for five which make 85
$85 \div 5 = 17$
The numbers are   15, 16, (17), 18, 19

Figure 5.4   Mathematical discoveries from a Year 4 class

dilemma – not wanting to give children text books which are written for much older children yet wanting to offer them more advanced experiences. Perhaps the above example offers some ideas on how to include advanced concepts within contexts which appeal to younger children.

Interdisciplinary enquiries

We think children learn best through being actively involved in the learning process and making as many connections as possible in their conceptual framework. Able pupils often grasp concepts and make connections very quickly. Using an inter-disciplinary approach we can make the learning contexts more interesting and challenging. When an activity has its starting point in one obvious subject area, the possibilities for making cross-curricular links should be explored.

'The Bees' Tribute', as can be seen in Figure 5.5 opposite was designed as a science-based project as part of the 'Bright Challenge' project. Its context of war was used by teachers to encourage research into history and geography. A bees' conference was made into role play in an English lesson. Editing and drafting as well desk-top publishing was used to prepare an article. Teachers who trialled this activity reported that a substantial amount of high quality work was produced by pupils in response to this project.

Incorporating 'higher order' thinking skills

A curriculum model which offers opportunities for higher levels of thinking, based on Bloom's Taxonomy, was introduced Chapter 4. A more recent list of what is involved in 'higher order' thinking, from Resnick (1987), may also be of interest to readers. Resnick maintains that higher order thinking should be available to children in schools, and for her higher order thinking

- is **non-algorithmic**. That is, the path of action is not fully specified in advance

- tends to be **complex**. The total path is not 'visible' from a single vantage (mentally speaking) point

- often yields **multiple solutions**, each with costs and benefits, rather than unique solutions

- involves **nuanced judgement** and interpretations

- involves the application of **multiple criteria**, which sometimes conflict with one another

- often involves **uncertainty**. Not everything that influences the task at hand is known

SCIENCE

The bees' tribute

During the first World War, on the battlefields of Flanders, many young soldiers lost their lives. When the shelling had stopped and the trenches were no longer in use, the grass began to grow again. Peace returned and so did the bees. Soon the blood-stained fields were decorated with red, flowering poppies. People thought this was so remarkable that the red poppy became a symbol of Remembrance Sunday, the day on which we remember those who died during the two World Wars. Yet without the work of many bees the poppies would not have multiplied and flourished. It is as though the bees have paid a tribute to the dead.

 Your challenge is to prepare an article for a new school magazine, explaining the 'bees' tribute'.

First you must find the answers to the following questions:

- *How was it possible for those poppies to appear and spread so fast?*

- *What role could the bees have played?*

To begin to understand these things you need to research:

- The parts of the poppy and their functions. What are the *sepals, petals, pistils, ovules, ovaries, pollen tubes?*

- The partnership between the bees and the poppies. What do the words *pollination* and *fertilization* mean? What attracts the bee to the flower, and what happens during these visits?

Figure 5.5   'The bee's tribute' (from *Bright Challenge*, (Casey and Koshy, 1995)

- involves **self-regulation** of the thinking process. We do not recognise higher order thinking in an individual when someone 'calls the plays' at every step

- involves **imposing meaning**: finding structure in apparent disorder

- is **effortful**. There is considerable mental work involved in the kinds of elaborations and judgements required.

Much of what Resnick has listed here has great significance in designing curriculum materials for higher ability able pupils. Many of the examples of activities we have included in this book do take Resnick's list into account. An interesting task for you to be engaged in before you leave this section is to think of one of your recent lessons and evaluate whether and how you may or may not have included these features of higher order thinking in your teaching.

Providing opportunities for individual enquiries

Previously, we discussed the role of motivation in the learning process. Many higher ability pupils are capable of independent learning and enquiry and they are quite often passionate about topics they are interested in. If one subscribes to Gardners' theory of Multiple Intelligences, pupils possess aptitudes in specific domains and these need to be nurtured. It may not always be possible to meet all their needs within the daily structure of the classroom time-table. Teachers often tell us about their guilt in not being able to find time for their most able pupils, partly because of the pressure of time and sometimes because they believe in the myth that the able can look after themselves. One of the ways of dealing with this is to look out for opportunities to encourage individual work. For example, if a pupil has a strong interest in the topic of coins, it makes sense to direct some of his or her classwork or homework towards researching that topic. One such instance was reported by a secondary school form teacher:

Matthew, one of my very able pupils, is passionate about coins. I only found this out by accident when I saw him show his impressive collection of coins to his friends, at break-time. I let all his teachers know about this. Several of his teachers encouraged him to pursue this interest through other lessons. The ultimate success for him was entering a museum competition. This was through the encouragement he received from his history teacher. The judges were so impressed by his entry that he was invited to go abroad and do a presentation to a National Museum.

For such success stories as Matthew's to happen, the teacher needs to play a significant role. Focusing on 'significant achievement' of pupils and target setting are very effective ways of achieving this. Clarke's (1996) series of books on how significant achievement can effectively be targeted at primary school level should make very useful reading (see the end of the book for more reading guidance).

Encouraging research skills

An enrichment activity designed by a group of Key Stage 2 teachers in Richmond LEA, shown in Figure 5.6 on page 74 is an example of encouraging pupils to accept opportunities for considerable research for pupils. A careful look at this activity shows how pupils can be encouraged to use scientific processes of considering evidence, identifying patterns and making predictions through collecting data for this project. It can be seen that the research which has to be carried out for this kind of activity is substantial. What is also evident is the way most pupils will be able to carry out this project at their own level, with the most able pupils in the class taking the investigation to a more sophisticated level of enquiry.

Offering potential for creative learning and thinking

The role of creativity in developing pupils' potential is one of the themes we have emphasised in previous chapters of this book. You may recall that there is support from theoretical models for the need to offer pupils opportunities for creative activity. In our experience, higher ability pupils often respond very positively to creative opportunities and produce some very original pieces of work. One activity we have trialled for our secondary English project entitled 'The Pharaoh's Ghost' produced some very exciting responses from 14 year-olds. The activity, as can be seen in Figure 5.7a on page 75 asks the pupils to imagine themselves to be Pharaohs and organise their own funerals. The most enthusiastic responses from higher ability pupils, such as the example in Figure 5.7b on page 76, in our experience often resulted from activities which were unusual and appealed to their creativity. This has been true of all age groups.

Encouraging pupil-evaluations

One of the features we stress strongly on our in-service course is the process of evaluation. Evaluations can take different forms. Self-evaluation promotes reflection on both the ideas used and the learning process itself. It helps pupils to set new targets, which in turn can often enhance their achievement. Peer group evaluations of projects and presentations can often stimulate much thinking among higher ability pupils, who often set high standards for themselves anyway.

Incorporating opportunities for using Information Technology

Information Technology, with its power, speed and sophisticated facilities, has much to offer the education of all pupils. In the case of higher ability pupils, Information Technology can play a very significant role. Programmes such as Logo and adventure programmes can challenge the most able pupils through problem

Planet Bong

What is it like on planet Bong?

You are an astronomer who has recently discovered a new planet in our solar system. It fits in with all the existing patterns in our solar system.

You are going to prepare a data sheet to present to other astronomers. You must include information about:

- *distance the planet is from the sun*

- *its temperature*

- *what it is made from*

- *the length of its year*

- *length of the day*

- *the number of moons it has*

- *the planets weather.*

Things to consider afterwards:
Does your planet have water?
Does it have oxygen?

Can you design a holiday brochure for your planet?
What does it look like?
Make a model.

Name: [   ]   Date: [   ]   page no.

Figure 5.6   'Planet Bong' – an activity encouraging research

2.2 The pharaoh's ghost

The practice of embalming the bodies of rulers of ancient Egypt, after their death and before placing them in a pyramid, has led to mummies now being on display in many museums around the world.

The Pharaohs believed in a form of life after death – hence the elaborate construction of the pyramids and the wealth of their contents. They were not to know of archaeologists coming into existence thousands of years later who would remove their *sarcophaguses* for display and historical interest. The pharaohs died believing that the Goddess Isis would protect them and that other goddesses residing in stars were fit companions for them.

Curiosity pursuit
Imagine you were a pharaoh in ancient Egypt. Try to collect information about the beliefs which influenced your preparations for death.

Why was your burial chamber in the shape of a pyramid? Did it have something to do with energy?

What was the role of stars and your belief in goddesses?

What kind of existence after death were you anticipating?

Now pretend that your mummified body is currently on display in a museum and that you were completely wrong about the kind of existence you would have after death. In fact, assume that you are a thinking and talking ghost wandering about in the Egyptology section of the museum.

Describe in prose or in a one act play, how you would enter into a dialogue with the visitors and the curator of the museum for the following purposes:

- *to try to explain to them how you came to arrange for your body to be embalmed after death.*
- *to try to understand why people came to just look at your body*
- *to try to complain about the lack of respect, shown by ordinary people, for the once mighty pharaoh.*
- *to try to convince a visiting lawyer that you had the freehold of the pyramid in which you were buried and so parliament would be lobbied to introduce legislation so that archaeologists responsible for your body being removed should be prosecuted for trespassing and grievous spiritual harm to your god-like existence after death.*

You may care to take out a summons of Anubis, the god of death, for misrepresentation of life after death, causing you to misguidedly channel considerable wealth into the building of your pyramid and the stock of its contents.

Figure 5.7a   'The Pharaoh's Ghost', from *Bright Challenge* (Casey and Koshy, 1997)

Life beyond death – a joyful yearning. Isis in the heavens as Sirius will be joined by me. The apex of my pyramid will gather infinite energy for my eternal bliss. Yet, what if I am duped. Isis becomes a phantom. My sarcophagus will be the bounty of thieves. I will reduce to dust and the goddesses, waiting for me in the stars, change into tantalising twinkles in the memory of my self-deceiving eyes.

Figure 5.7b An extract of writing from a Year 9 pupil from the viewpoint of the Pharoah

solving and posing further challenges themselves. Figure 5.8 opposite shows evidence of a powerful learning experience for a higher ability pupil aged 9.

Databases and spreadsheets can often enable higher ability pupils to be engaged in sophisticated methods of collecting, processing and interpreting data. The beginnings of five year-old Nishal's work on correlation of the size of different parts of the human body using a spreadsheet, as shown on Figure 5.9 on page 78, is an example of what can be achieved. Nishal produced a whole folder for this project over a period of three weeks. Desk-top publishing can enhance the quality of presentation of work as well as encourage the production of creative posters, journals and books. We recently saw two very able children given the responsibility of displaying summaries of library books outside and inside the library. Having CD-Roms with instant access to encyclopaedias and other factual books and the facility of printing out selected sections, can be extremely useful resources for enriching the learning experiences of higher ability pupils. Koshy and Dodds (1995) list ideas for using IT in the primary school and this may provide a useful reference.

My Logo diary

Drawing a rocket

It took me six hours to draw this rocket. Miss showed me a picture of a rocket and I made an outline of it.

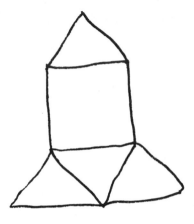

It looks so simple, but when you start programming, you realise there are lots of things to work out, like angles and turns and so on. Everytime I thought I cracked it, new 'bugs' (that is what I call the mistakes now, after talking to Miss Crass) started to come up.

I was not going to give up. Most of the time I thought I cracked it and tried to draw a picture, it turned out to be different to what I thought it was going to be like. I used to wake up in the middle of the night thinking about new ways to try. Finally I got there and felt very happy although it was very very hard.

Figure 5.8 A Logo programmer's diary (child aged 9)

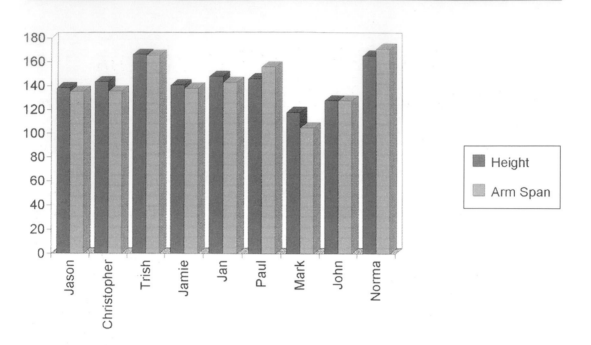

Figure 5.9 Investing correlation using a spreadsheet by Nishal, aged 5

One of the greatest advantages of using IT, in our experience, is that it supports groups of children in some special categories. For example, very young children who are capable of producing very sophisticated ideas, such as the piece of work of a six year-old on 'Puddles' in Figure 5.10 opposite, whose spelling skills have not developed as fast as her stunning thinking capability, could be encouraged to word-process. Having access to wordprocessing gives opportunities for pupils who have difficulties with the physical process of writing, but are still very capable of producing powerful ideas.

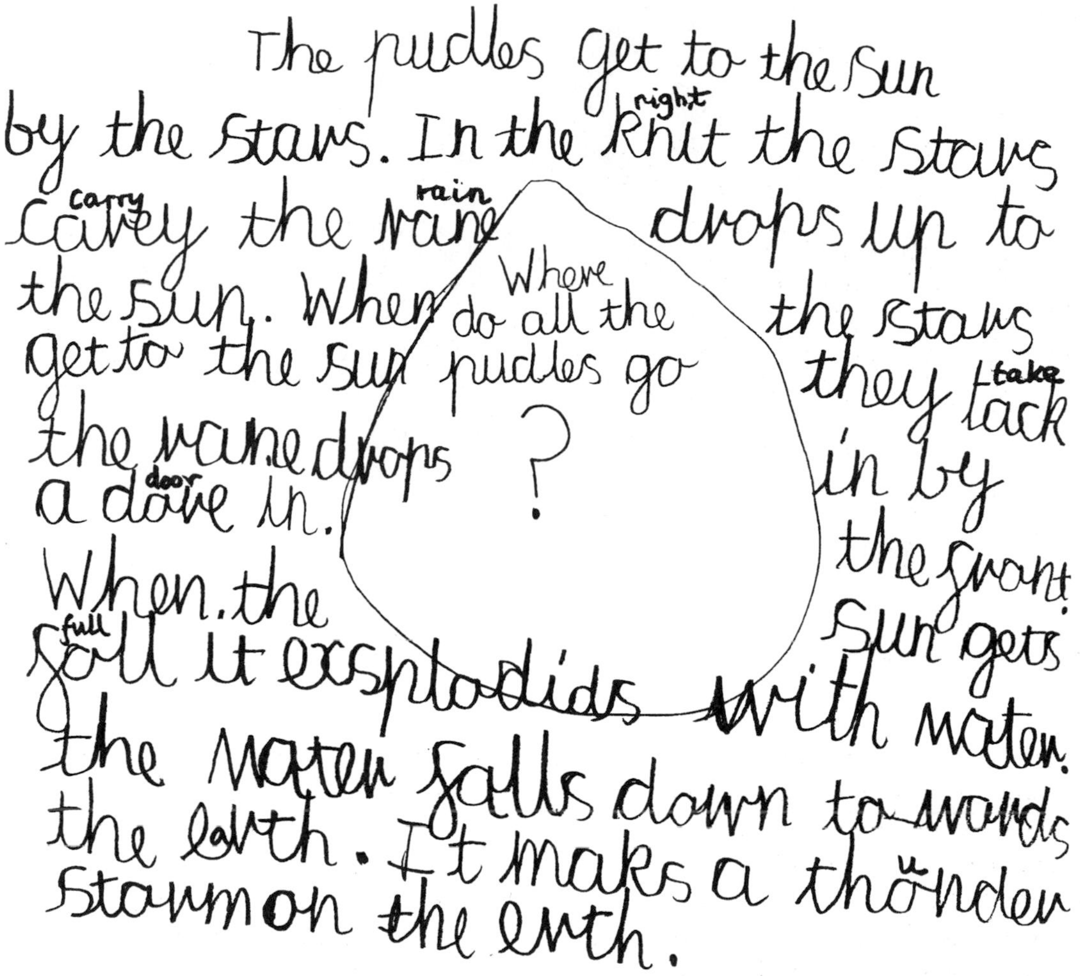

The pudles get to the Sun by the stars. In the *right* knit the stars *carry* the *rain* ~~rane~~ drops up to the sun. When *Where* do all the puddles go the stars get to the sun they *take* ~~tack~~ the rane drops a *door* ~~dore~~ in. ? in by

When the *full* ~~foll~~ it exsplodeds with water. the water falls down towards the earth. It maks a thönder storm on the erth. the front Sun gets

Figure 5.10 'Where do all the puddles go?' by Katherine, aged 6

Summary

To summarise then, we believe that the quality of teaching is one of the most important factors which determines the realisation of potential of all pupils. Higher ability children are no exception. In this chapter we have provided you with some principles for designing curriculum materials, based on our experience of working with higher ability pupils for a number of years. Providing a Square Deal for our higher ability pupils is every teachers' wish; this chapter may have provided you with some more practical strategies for achieving that aim. We have always placed much emphasis on the role of task commitment, motivation, environmental stimulation and creativity in creating the most suitable conditions for nurturing talent.

CHAPTER 6

Making a Difference to Educating Higher Ability Pupils

In the previous chapters of this book we have discussed aspects which we consider to be the most relevant to making the most effective educational provision for higher ability pupils in our schools. The need for such consideration for the education of higher ability pupils is emphasised by many agencies such as HMI (1992, p. vii) who told us that:

Very able pupils in maintained primary and secondary schools are often insufficiently challenged by the work they are set.

Although the review of HMI findings where the above quotation appears uses the term 'very able' to refer to the top 5% of the ability range, we have much evidence to suggest that provision for a wider range of the higher ability segment of the continuum has been a neglected area for a very long time. Our own research and OfSTED inspection reports bear testimony to that. One of the main aims of writing this book has been to share our thinking and strategies with teachers, as well as others who are interested in making a difference to educating able children. We hope you have enjoyed reading the book and that through your interactive journey with us feel you are now able to meet the challenge of teaching higher ability pupils with more understanding and confidence.

In this chapter we take a careful look at what factors can make a difference to the provision of able children and make some suggestions. Among the factors which have helped teachers, two are worth special mention. One is the provision of school-based in-service sessions where issues can be reflected on in the context of one's own school. The second is having a school policy specifically targeting provision for able pupils. Both must involve the whole staff however long it takes for members to feel they 'own' this responsibility, as well as develop their shared understanding of what it is all about. In the concluding sections of the book we provide you with some guidelines on how to organise in-service sessions and give you an opportunity to look at some school policies which exist in different phases of schooling.

HMI (1992, p. 16) provides us with a useful list of 'features' which help to contribute to high quality provision for able pupils:

- a high level of commitment by the head and, in secondary schools, the senior management to the education of the very able

- the involvement of the majority of members in planning programmes for the very able as well as appropriate in-service training

- the presence of an active co-ordinator

- close attention to the needs of the individual pupil through differentiation of tasks

- careful monitoring of individual progress

- teachers with a deep understanding of their subjects

- high expectations of what pupils can achieve

- appropriate choice of resources

- pupils being encouraged to think for themselves, to ask questions, to take some responsibility for their own learning and to contribute ideas

- variation in pace, teaching style and classroom organisation

- a stimulating environment

- good LEA support

We have attempted to focus on much of the contents of the above list in the preceding chapters of this book.

When we asked 150 teachers who have attended our longer in-service courses to list what they thought had made the most difference to practical provision in their schools the following emerged as the top five:

- The existence of a co-ordinator with responsibility for the education of able children

- Having a school policy specifically targeting provision for able children

- School based in-service

- Some input on differentiating the curriculum

- Clear guidance on identification and recording of identified talent

In the following sections we will deal with the items in the above list. First we will discuss the role of the co-ordinator. Then we will focus on how to design a school policy. In order to design an effective policy, teachers need to have an understanding of the various issues relating to higher ability pupils. This, we believe, can often be achieved by arranging a series of meetings or workshops within one's own school. We will provide you with some suggestions on how to conduct some school-based sessions as part of the policy-making process. The last two items will be incorporated into the sessions.

The role of the co-ordinator

Increasingly, in both primary and secondary schools, the special needs co-ordinator is being asked to take on the needs of 'able' children as an additional responsibility. Although it makes sense for one person to co-ordinate the responsibility for both ends of special needs, we would like to make it very clear that the special needs co-ordinator will need much support to take on this additional responsibility. The needs of the pupils at the two ends of the ability continuum are different in significant ways. In some schools, the responsibility for able pupils and other special needs pupils are given to two separate people who work together. This is often an effective strategy.

In secondary schools where we have felt there was effective provision, co-ordinators were given sufficient time and opportunities to attend courses and conferences so that they could develop their own understanding before having to provide leadership to others. In both primary and secondary schools where subject co-ordinators worked in collaboration with subject teams, curriculum provision seemed to be of higher quality.

Responsibilities of the co-ordinator

In schools where the responsibility for able pupils was specifically given to one teacher, the following were included in their responsibilities

- raising colleagues' awareness of the need for specifically addressing the needs of able pupils

- setting up identification and monitoring strategies

- attend in-service sessions, organised both by LEA and others to develop own expertise

- set up a resource area of books and other materials

- arrange school-based in-service sessions

- attend some meetings of year-groups and subject teams

- develop identification strategies for different curriculum areas

- liaise with support organisations and share information about facilities offered by them with colleagues and parents

- dissemination of good practice

- take a lead in designing the school policy and monitor its effectiveness

- support colleagues with effective curriculum planning strategies

- individual counselling for any referred pupils and their parents who need support

- oversee the organisation of school-based enrichment clubs and other activities

The above list is long and this strongly implies that the responsibility is very demanding and challenging. Much support and recognition needs to be given to the co-ordinator.

Developing a whole-school policy for educating higher ability pupils

A national survey conducted by us in primary schools, which is currently being analysed, showed that only a small percentage had a school policy of any kind for 'provision for able children', although we have had indicators that many schools would like to have one. We have often been asked if we knew of any published policies with a view to 'getting a copy' or to buying one. As with all policies, we strongly believe that for any school policy to be effective all members of staff, teaching and support staff, need to have some involvement in designing it. The nature of the involvement may differ due to time constraints and other pressures, but every one who has to implement the policy must have an understanding of the issues dealt with in the policy. We have visited schools which had 'policies' for the education of the very able pupils in teachers' files, written by the co-ordinator, but which had not been read by the rest of the staff. Our own belief is that the time spent on collectively designing policies is well spent. Issues relating to higher ability children are complex and contentious; teachers need time for discussion and reflection before a policy can be effectively designed and implemented.

Making a start with designing a school policy

If a school has a named person who is responsible for the educational provision of able children, it makes sense for that person to co-ordinate the writing of the policy. Remember the whole process takes time. It is important to generate principles through substantial discussion and debate. We suggest the following in-service sessions as a possible sequence to assist you to timetable a programme of action. Obviously, each school will have its own agenda and would need to adapt these sessions to suit their needs. For each session, the proposed aims, procedure and questions are provided.

Session 1   In order to be able to say 'these are our able pupils'; what do you need to be sure of?

Aims
The main aim of this introductory session is to highlight the general issues surrounding identification of ability. During this session many controversial issues should come up for discussion. It sets the scene for the teacher to start developing a personal understanding of the relevant features and controversies in relation to the education of higher ability pupils.

Procedure
Give a copy of the case studies from Chapter 1 (or use your own) to the teachers, in pairs or threes. While reading these the group should make a list of questions and concerns. After a reasonable time collect all the contributions on a flip chart.

Some schools may decide to ask teachers to list the issues buzzing in their heads surrounding 'able children' without referring to case studies first. In either case your list of issues and questions may look like the one below, from an actual session:

I don't really understand all these terms – able, very able, gifted, talented
Why such variety? Why can't we use one word?

Do you need specialist, gifted, teachers to teach the brightest kids?

I have attended three one-day conferences on able children so far. I know we have a lot of bright kids. Not one of the conferences has offered me any solid pieces of advice on how to provide for them, in a practical sense. You need more than a day to get your thinking going.

I have never had a 'gifted' pupil in my class in the last thirty years of teaching, I have taught many bright ones

It does make sense to teach all the very able ones together with 'clever' teachers

How do you know how able a child is?

All the bright ones I know are lazy pupils, is that general?

One of my parents keeps asking what support is available in our school. I haven't got a clue

As a Year 7 teacher I need to know whether I should identify the 'all-round gifted children' or look for 'subject-specific' giftedness

After transferring the list onto a flip chart ask groups of three to choose the questions and issues (one at a time). Discuss and jot down the group's collective thoughts or solutions for each of them. Each group may record their chosen issue like this:

How do you measure how bright a child is?
It is possible to have a psychologist administer an IQ test which gives a figure which denotes potential. The practicality of every child being tested is 'impossible'. In any case what help would a figure be to us? We have no solution to this particular question, except to say that you do not need to know 'how able' a child is. What matters is that you realise that a particular child has higher potential to be engaged in more 'challenging learning' and we have to provide it.

The group then shares its thoughts with the large group. Then ask everyone to take two minutes and make a note of two to three issues which have made an impact on their thinking, so far, about aspects of identification of higher ability pupils.

In preparation for the second session, it would be useful to ask all those who attended the first session to read Chapter 1 of this book.

Session 2   Identification of able children

Aims
This session is designed to provide more insight into the complexity of the identification process and generate some ideas on how schools can use some of the structures already available to identify able pupils. It also provides an opportunity to discuss identification criteria.

Ask the teachers to think for a few minutes and construct a profile of the most able pupil they have in their class or have taught in the last few years, and record all their characteristics, in words or short phrases, which come to mind. A spider diagram may be shown as a model of this.

When everyone has completed this task, ask three or four people to share their lists before writing down all the features recorded by the group without repeating ideas. A list should emerge. The following is an example of what emerged as a list in one secondary school.

Characteristics of higher ability pupils

- 'bone' idle

- learns very fast

- knows more than me

- brilliant at everything

- hates being told 'something is not done right'

- constantly 'screws' up unfinished work and starts again

- shows amazing general knowledge

- does not enjoy writing, but likes debates

- very sensitive and magnanimous

- worries about the world's problems

- always looks bored

- mum told me she had him tested and has the highest IQ recorded, then I started taking note.

Allow discussions and ask for explanations of what has been recorded. There should be some lively discussions and debates arising out of these.

It is likely that one of the questions which comes up is to do with the dilemma of ability being a 'general' term or whether it described aptitudes in specific areas. The co-ordinator or a volunteer can make a presentation of Howard Gardner's Multiple Intelligences theory and draw everyone's attention to how he describes *seven* types of intelligences.

Share both the identification list from Chapter 2 and the checklist based on Gardner's principles with everyone and let them take the checklist away. Ask each member to record any changes in their perceptions of their pupils, in general terms or in specific areas, and bring them back to the next session. Secondary schools may find it particularly useful to compile a list of what constitutes high ability in subject areas.

In preparation for the next session ask the members to read Chapter 3

Session 3 Provision

Aims
In this session we begin to think about curriculum provision for higher ability pupils.

Procedure
The co-ordinator starts with a presentation (about 20 minutes) on how to plan the curriculum, paying attention to 'higher levels of thinking' from Bloom's Taxonomy with the help of your own examples or those from Chapter 4 of this book. This should be followed by a practical workshop (in year groups or subject groups). Each group chooses a topic and lists a set of questions for each of the six levels. They also suggest how they would plan a lesson based on the ideas from the section on higher levels of thinking. Share their findings. It would be useful if the specific lesson planned is put up for examination by everyone, evaluating why it may or may not be suitable for high ability pupils.

Members are asked to read Chapters 4 and 5 before session 4.

Session 4 Where are we now?

Aims
Having considered what constitutes ability and what needs to be done, it is now appropriate to target this session to plan action.

Procedure
Ask teachers to read a copy of the OfSTED report extract in Chapter 1, which provides a useful list of what needs to be done in the school to make sure that effective provision is made for higher ability pupils. This can be done in groups. Ask them to discuss and make notes on each item on the list, to find out where the school is with regard to each aspect. An example is:

To the question

Are there references to the needs of very able children in the subject schemes of work?

the following was recorded by a group of primary school teachers.

No, we have never thought of able children in 'subject' categories – neither in the assessment or provision. We have some reference to investigations being suitable for the able mathematicians, in our maths policy. That is too vague, no-one takes any notice.

We need to look at all our policies and now, taking Gardner's ideas and our own observations into account, we need to make a list to guide us in identifying talent in different subject areas and make suggestions for provision.

Before the end of the session members of each group shares their thoughts with the larger group enabling the leader to compile a list of what needs to be done. This is good preparation for beginning to think of writing a policy.

Session 5   What should be in the policy?

Aims
The aim is to consider what a policy should include and what form it takes.

Procedure
The leader or co-ordinator presents the list of what the staff decided, in the previous session, were the needs of the school giving some indicators as to what should be included in the policy.

Ask each member of the group to write down the heading they would like to see in a policy and to justify what they mean by each of the chosen headings. Collate the list, discarding repeats.

The following list contains some broad headings and questions which may be usefully shared with members before the headings for your policy are finalised.

Rationale

- Do we need a policy for the identification and provision for higher ability pupils in our school?

- If we do, should it be a separate policy statement, or be incorporated into the school's special needs policy?

- What is the general context of the policy within our school's ethos and philosophy?

Aims

- What main aims do we need to set for educating our most able pupils?

- Do our aims include personal, social and educational development of the pupils?

- Do our aims reflect equity?

Identification of ability

- What do we mean by higher ability pupils?

- What criteria are used for the identification of higher ability pupils?

- Do we use all available information in deciding the nature of provision?

- How flexible is our identification process?

- Are we taking the multiple talents of our pupils into account?

- What forms of recording do we use to support the recognition of high ability within the identified group?

- Are there mechanisms provided for continuity and progression?

Provision

- How do we intend to make provision through curriculum planning?

- What strategies are being used for effective differentiation?

- What kinds of organisational strategies and teaching style are being used?

- Do we intend to involve outside agencies?

- Are there opportunities for pupils to develop individual interests?

- What arrangements are made for catering for pupils who show high ability in specific subjects?

- Does the school operate an enrichment projects scheme as part of the curriculum or as extra-curricular activities?

- If yes, how is the membership of the scheme decided?

Resources

- Does the school have a co-ordinator to monitor the implementation of the policy?

- What are the co-ordinator's responsibilities?

- Are there any specially designed commercially produced materials available in the school?

Review and monitoring of the policy

- How will this policy be monitored?

- How often will it be reviewed?

- How will the staff be supported to implement the policy?

Before the close of this session ask each group to take two headings from the list and make some notes about what should be included in each of the items. All the members give their notes to the co-ordinator at the end of this session, who will undertake to put it together (typed) so that a draft policy can be considered.

Session 6   Getting ready for action

Aims
During this session a draft policy, perhaps still in note form, is presented for discussion.

Procedure
The draft policy is presented offering everyone a chance to have a say in what changes may be needed, as well as consider what structures need to be put in place for making the policy work. It may be useful for all the members to look at the two examples of school policies, given below, before the final draft is put together.

It is useful to make it clear to all those who attended the meetings that the policy is still in draft form and its success and effectiveness will need to be monitored and reviewed after it has been tried out for a reasonable period. It may be useful to include the addresses of the supporting agencies and resources listed at the end of this book.

Examples of two school policies

A school policy for the identification and provision for higher ability pupils within a secondary school

The context

All the students in the school are valued for their individual strengths and abilities whether this be in a core curriculum area or in any other area. We decided to design a separate policy for higher ability pupils in this school for the following reasons:

- We have a separate policy for special needs of the slower learners in the school. We believe that higher ability pupils also have special needs and we feel it is right that their needs are met within the structure of our organisation

- The staff feel that some targeting of resources is needed to give a high profile to meeting the needs of able children which has not hitherto been attended to

Definitions of ability

We recognise that it is difficult to work to water-tight definitions of what constitutes a higher ability student. We are aware of the numerous terms used to describe higher ability, and for the purpose of this document we adopt a definition that higher ability pupils may display aptitudes either in general or in specific areas.

According to the HMI review (1992) entitled 'The Education of Very Able Children in Maintained Schools' approximately 10 to 12% of all school children may be high achievers in one subject area only and 5% of the school population may be high achievers in one or more subject areas. We are aware of the existence of IQ tests, which measure potential, although these are only administered when we feel a psychologist's report is needed for specific purposes.

All the staff are made aware of the recent recognition by educationists and psychologists that the concept of the existence of Multiple Intelligences put forward by Howard Gardner is a useful way of both assessing abilities and the nurturing of these abilities. The theory of Multiple Intelligences acknowledges the possibility that a person may be a high achiever in one or more specific area. The seven intelligences listed by Howard Gardner are:

- Musical intelligence

- Linguistic intelligence

- Logico-mathematical intelligence

- Interpersonal intelligence

- Bodily kinesthetic intelligence
- Spatial intelligence
- Intra-personal intelligence

We strive to identify all types of intelligence and nurture them. Efforts are made to provide experiences for pupils to develop all seven kinds of intelligence although the student may only exhibit special aptitudes in one or more areas.

Identification

Consistent with the adoption of a Multiple Intelligences approach, each department is provided opportunities to devise their own identification criteria. Subject-related checklists are developed by subject teams which are used in conjunction with test results, reports from previous form teacher or school, communications from parents and all other mechanisms available. All members of staff are also provided with a general checklist of characteristics of higher ability pupils, which may be a useful reference point.

We agreed that the most effective way of identifying higher ability pupils is through observing them engaged in learning an enjoyable and challenging curriculum. A dull and repetitive curriculum is unlikely to provide indicators of higher ability.

Flexibility is to be maintained at all times. There are many instances of high ability being masked for all sorts of reasons. Language problems, deprived home background, lack of confidence and the fear of being given 'extra' work can often stand in the way of teacher identification; therefore information from multiple sources on pupils' ability should be sought.

The school keeps a register of 'special aptitudes and abilities' of its pupils. All personal achievements are included in the Records of Achievement.

Provision

Differentiation by task and by outcome are practised in all departments. Seminars are arranged for staff from different departments to share strategies and their relative effectiveness.

Staff are made aware of the need to incorporate higher levels of thinking through familiarisation with Bloom's Taxonomy and consideration of higher order questioning skills. Each department employs its own methodology for differentiating the curriculum and the pupils are provided training in what experts use as their methodology in their professional role.

Enrichment projects
Enrichment clusters are organised in school time in a few areas – music, chess, photography, mathematics, technology and creative writing. Membership is not restricted, although pupils who are very talented are strongly encouraged to participate. Outside experts and some parents offer help during these sessions, for professional input. In addition to these enrichment clusters, pupils are given information on courses at the local university or about evening classes in their area.

The co-ordinator
The school has a co-ordinator for provision for 'high ability' pupils. Her responsibility is to keep the documentation up to date, co-ordinate team meetings and disseminate the latest thinking and research in this area of education.

Parental involvement
We recognise the important part played by parents in both identification and provision for the most able pupils. Parents are asked, at the time of their children starting at this school, to list any special strengths and talents. This information is circulated amongst all the teachers. Parents are also invited to take part in all extra enrichment activities provided for the pupils. A list of outside agencies and support available in different areas is made accessible to parents who ask for extra support.

Monitoring the policy
It is the responsibility of the co-ordinator to monitor the effectiveness of this policy through a range of mechanisms, which include administering a questionnaire, and conducting individual interviews with representatives from subject teams.

A school policy for the identification and provision for higher ability pupils within a primary school

Introduction
The school endeavours to:

develop the whole child intellectually, socially and emotionally and it is within this context that a special policy is being devised for the recognition and provision for the most able pupils in our school. This is consistent with our equal opportunities policy that all pupils should be given opportunities to develop their full potential.

We recognise that higher ability pupils have special needs which need to be recognised and action taken.

This policy was designed by the staff collaboratively over a period of five months and compiled by the special needs co-ordinator. What is listed here has been subjected to much debate and deliberation.

Identification

Able and exceptionally able pupils may show particular strengths in any of the following:

- physical talent
- general intellectual ability
- creative thinking
- leadership qualities
- artistic ability
- specific academic aptitudes

These strengths are identified through a range of methods:

- Teacher assessment
- NFER tests which are administered yearly
- SATS results
- Parents' comments
- Nursery entry profile
- Information from previous teacher/school
- Awareness raising checklist of characteristics

We accept that all children are different and able children are also unlikely to exhibit an accepted pattern of behaviour. It is useful to remember that disruptive behaviour and aggressiveness may be the result of able pupils not being challenged and valued – though such behaviour is not an indicator of high ability.

Provision

A number of strategies are adopted:

1 During planning meetings questions and challenges are devised in the context of the National Curriculum with open-ended tasks.

2 A range of teaching styles are adopted which accept that higher ability children may have their own individual learning styles.

3 All the class topics are looked at within the framework of Bloom's Taxonomy and specific projects are planned.

4 A bank of resources, both commercially produced as well as those developed within the school, are stored in the filing cabinet. Some commentary regarding their use and effectiveness is included within these resources.

5 Subject policies include criteria for identification of talent.

6 Specific teaching strategies are adopted within the normal classroom. Acceleration is provided for some pupils who are moved up a year if parents, teachers and pupils all see this as a useful move.

7 Opportunities are provided for individual work and for specially planned home-work.

8 Pupils who display exceptional ability are provided with opportunities to have specialist help either from subject co-ordinators or mentors, if the need arises.

9 Special efforts are made to recognise pupils' talents and create the right ethos in school where being academically able is accepted in the same way as sporting and musical or other talents are accepted.

Staff development

The co-ordinator keeps staff informed of developments within the LEA and with national networks. Every member of staff is provided with a booklet which contains a copy of the policy, addresses of support organisations and resources.

Policy review

This will be carried out every year with a view to modifying strategies, adding to resources and providing in-service support.

Summary

A word of caution here. Considering that the policies of other schools provide some help in devising your own policy, we cannot over-emphasise the need for all the members of a schools' staff to understand what is included in the policy. For example, if reference is made to 'providing higher-order questioning skills' it is only common sense that teachers who have to implement the policy have some first-hand experience of acquiring such skills.

Most teachers who have worked with us have appreciated having a list of organisations which support the education of able pupils, as well as a booklist. These are provided in the following pages.

Useful addresses

The Brunel Able Children's Education centre (BACE)
School of Education
Brunel University
300 St Margaret's Road
Twickenham
Middlesex TW1 1PT

The support Society for Children of High Intelligence
PO Box 4222
London SE22 8XG

Gift
5 Ditton Court Road
Westcliff-on-Sea
Essex SS0 7HG

National Association for Able Children in Education (NACE)
Room L6
Westminster College
Oxford OX2 9AT

National Association for Gifted Children (NAGC)
Park Campus
Boughton Green Road
Northampton NN2 7AL

Some subject specialist organisations

Mathematics

London Mathematical Society
Burlington House
Piccadilly
London W1V 4AH

The Association of Teachers of Mathematics
7 Shaftesbury Street
Derby DE3 8YB

Mathematics Association
259 London Road
Leicester LE2 3BE

English

The English Association
The Vicarage
Priory Gardens
Bedford Park
London W4 1TT

Science & Technology

Association for Science Education
College Lane
Hatfield
Herts AL10 9AA

Information Technology

The National Council for Educational
Technology (NCET)
Sir Willimas Lyons Road
Science Park
University of Warwick
Coventry CV4 7EZ

Bibliography

Bloom, B.S. (1956) *Taxonomy of Educational Objectives*, vol. 1. Longman.

Bloom, B.S. (1995) *Developing Talent in Young People*. New York: Ballantine Books.

Casey, R. and Koshy, V. (1995) *Bright Challenge*. Stanley Thornes.

Casey, R. and Koshy, V. (1997) *Bright Challenge: Key Stage 3*. Stanley Thornes.

Clarke, S. series ed (1996) *Tracking Significant Achievement in Mathematics*. London: Hodder and Stoughton.

Denton, C. and Postlewaithe, K. (1985) *Able Children*. NFER-Nelson.

Eyre, D. and Marjoram, T. (1990) *Enriching and Extending the National Curriculum*. Kogan Page.

Freeman, J. (1991) *Gifted Children Growing Up*. Cassell.

Freeman, J., Span, P. and Wagner, H. (eds) (1996) *Actualising Talent*. Cassell.

Gagne, F. (1985) 'Giftedness and talent: Re-examining a re-examination of the definitions', in *Gifted Children Quarterly*, 29, pp. 103–12.

Gardner, H. (1983) *Frames of Mind*. New York: Basic Books.

Gardner, H. (1993) *Multiple Intelligences*. New York: Basic Books.

Gardner, H. (1995) *Creating Creativity* in Times Educational Supplement, 6 January.

George, D. (1992) *The Challenge of the Able Child*. David Fulton Publishers.

HMI (1992) *The Education of Very Able Children in Maintained Schools*. HMSO.

Kerry, T. (1983) *Finding and Helping the Able Child*. Croom Helm.

Koshy, V. and Dodds, P. (1995) *Making IT Work for You – Information Technology Across the Primary Curriculum*. Stanley Thornes.

Leyden, S. (1985) *Helping Children of Exceptional Ability*. Croom Helm.

Montgomery, D. (1996) *Educating the Able*. Cassell.

Monks, F.J. (1992) 'Development of gifted children: The issue of identification and programming' in Monks, F.J. and Peters, W. *Talent for the Future*. Assery/Maastrict: Van Gorcum.

OfSTED (1993) *Exceptionally Able Children*. DFE.

Ogilvie, E. (1973) *Gifted Children in Primary Schools*. Macmillan.

Parnes, S.J. (1982) 'Education and creativity' in Vernon, P.E. (ed.) *Creativity*. Penguin Books.

Povey, R. (ed.) (1980) *Educating the Gifted Child*. New York: Harper & Row.

Renzulli, J. (1994) *Schools for Talent Development*. Creative Learning Press, PO Box 320, Mansfield Centre, CT 06250.

Renzulli, J. and Reis, S. (1985) *The Schoolwide Enrichment Model.* Creative Learning Press, PO Box 320, Mansfield Centre, CT 06250.

Resnick, L.B. (1987) *Education and Learning to Think.* Washington: National Academy Press.

Schools Update (1994) Spring 1994. DFE publication.

Sternberg, R.J. and Davidson, J.C. (eds) *Concepts of Giftedness.* Cambridge University Press.

Straker, A. (1983) *Mathematics for Gifted Pupils.* Longman.

Wallace, A. (1986) *The Prodigy.* Macmillan.

Index